Felix Velarde started one of the world's first web design agencies, then had a high-profile, twenty-year career as a serial entrepreneur and CEO. Along the way he made every mistake a founder and leader can make.

In 2014 Felix retired as CEO of a marketing services group and headed off to Burning Man. When he came back, he started helping companies who wanted to scale fast. Many of these companies have become market leaders, and several have sold, making their owners millions.

Felix co-created what *Forbes* has described as one of the world's ten most influential websites. He has been the subject of a BBC documentary, won many of the world's biggest creative and marketing awards and taught on the MBA program at Hult International, one of the world's best business schools. He is married to the actress Inna Bagoli and lives in London.

Praise for *Scale at Speed*:

'There are many business books that talk about what other companies have done in the past, but it's not often you get a step-by-step guide on how to grow your business from someone who has done it many times already. *Scale at Speed* is relevant, practical and essential for all entrepreneurs looking to grow their business'

Ronan Gruenbaum, Dean and Professor of Practice,
Hult International Business School

'Felix has distilled some of the best strategies he's learnt over twenty-five years of leading businesses of varying sizes into an easy-to-read framework. He expertly lays out the journey a business needs to undertake to scale. He breaks it down into digestible steps, allowing you to achieve your goals via well-structured frameworks and engaging stories along the way. I highly recommend you read this book to help you triple your business in two years, as many of his clients have, without stressing your employees or creating burnout'

Andrew Ellis, founder, Like Minds

'This is a must-read book ... [it] sparks ideas and gives you a framework to propel business growth ... This is not a book of fancy words and empty promises; it is a book written by someone who has been there and done it, has the battle scars to prove it and is prepared to share the secrets of that success with others'

Margaret Manning OBE, entrepreneur, diversity advocate
and former chair of the UK-ASEAN Business Council

'Felix Velarde has been advising People Centered Internet through the transition to my chairmanship from our founding chair, Vint Cerf. Our mission is to make the world a better place for all – and as a global organisation we need to be highly effective. The tools and principles he describes in detail in *Scale at Speed* have proven practical, sound and achievable at every step. Read this book, you won't regret it'

Mei Lin Fung, chair and co-founder, People Centered Internet

Scale at Speed

How to Triple the Size of Your Business and Build a Superstar Team

Felix Velarde

....

A How To book

ROBINSON

ROBINSON

First published in Great Britain in 2021
by Robinson.

This paperback edition published in 2023
by Robinson.

10 9 8 7 6 5

A CIP catalogue record for this book
is available from the British Library.

ISBN: 978-1-47214-588-8

Typeset in Sentinel and Scala Sans
by Ian Hughes.

Printed and bound in Great Britain by Clays
Ltd, Elcograf S.p.A.

Papers used by Robinson are from well-
managed forests and other responsible
sources.

Robinson
An imprint of
Little, Brown Book Group
Carmelite House
50 Victoria Embankment
London EC4Y 0DZ

An Hachette UK Company
www.hachette.co.uk

www.littlebrown.co.uk

How To Books are published by
Robinson, an imprint of Little, Brown
Book Group. We welcome proposals
from authors who have first-hand
experience of their subjects. Please set
out the aims of your book, its target
market and its suggested contents in an
email to howto@littlebrown.co.uk.

To all the pioneers, difference-makers
and visionaries, this book

To Inna, my heart

Contents

Foreword

Growing a business is easy once you've done it several times. You will have made all your mistakes and learned from them. You will know how to identify and motivate superstars without the tedious trial and error. You will get an exceptional price when you sell. Whether your staff number ten people or a thousand people, your business is a rocket on rails.

This book is for entrepreneurs and senior executives who wish it could be that easy. For those who are still struggling with integrating everything they've read and learned into a single, simple management framework. For you – definitely – if you want a simple system that brings your team together around a clearly articulated vision and helps you deliver fast growth.

In my twenty-five-year career as a pioneering founder, CEO and chairperson I've been involved in numerous trade sales. I've had one company go bust, and others come perilously close. I've made tens of millions in sales for my companies, and been responsible for teams making sales worth much, much more. I have made every rookie error and a fair few sophisticated mistakes. I've spent years learning from others, including the founders and CEOs of multinational conglomerates, tiny startups, famous SMEs and nascent tech giants.

The lessons I learned along the way became the experiments applied at my own businesses. They were tested, adapted and honed, then made accessible and practical. The resulting processes of rapid growth were built to be handed over to those who came afterwards.

In 2014 I stepped down as CEO of The Conversation Group and as chair of Underwired – which I had sold, bought back, doubling its turnover in a year, and later sold again. I became part of Vint Cerf and

Mei Lin Fung's People-Centered Internet and started going to Burning Man.

Since then I've chaired a wide range of agencies, startups and tech companies. Each of them has used the frameworks in this book. Their average growth rate has been 164 per cent in the first year. Today most of the companies we work with double or triple in size in their first eighteen to twenty-four months of applying the *Scale at Speed* formula. The process is simple, practical, unifying and strategic. It brings teams together and motivates superstars. It provides coherence in the senior team and clarity and vision for the company. It enables very rapid expansion without top-down pressure.

Each year some of these companies sell for significantly more than the market average. Many owners realise they don't want to sell; they find renewed enthusiasm in turning their business around and making it seriously profitable. They all love the process.

So why this book? I've taught these processes to hundreds of businesses, mostly independent, mostly owner-managed. One thing I can say for sure is that most entrepreneurs operate in a vacuum: it's lonely at the top of a business. There is nobody to tell you how it works. And people can waste years of their lives learning by trial and error.

It's exhilarating and fun during the ups, but frustrating, soul-destroying and no fun at all during the downs. Wouldn't it be wonderful if you could smooth it out so your family can enjoy the ride with you rather than having to be there for you when it's all going wrong again?

This book is a guide to how to make being a founder and a leader fun again, so that you get back to that state of excitement and inspiration and love for it all. It's a common-sense guide to some of the basic processes of rapid growth; to simple, relevant, good management; to the shortcuts that will help you avoid painful mistakes. You will discover how to implement these battle-hardened frameworks and accelerate your company to reach your goals and achieve your ambitions.

The formula for growth really is a formula for success. It is exceptionally accessible, and it delivers. Whether your company is losing money and needs to be turned around, or is already highly successful and you are determined to triple its revenue, this framework can be applied fast. It will have an immediate transformative effect, yet last for years. I want you to have it.

Introduction

One day's journey

I had always wanted to see the Himalayas, so I decided to go walking for a month, to see incredible views and be inspired by the beauty of nature at its most imposing. When I booked my trekking trip, the travel agency advised me to spend six months preparing with long walks in the English countryside. Each week the distance and difficulty was to be increased, so that by the time my trip came round I'd be fit for a trek around the Himalayan trails of Nepal.

As usual with these things, my social and work life got in the way a little. The only walk I took ended up being the weekend before the flight.

With a vision in my head of Annapurna South (though on this hazy day I couldn't yet see it), I stepped off the bus in the valley to be met by a guide. He took my bulging rucksack, leaving me with walking sticks and a flask, and we walked along the valley floor for a little while. After an hour we sat on a bench and he said, 'OK, we're going to walk for an hour up a gentle slope, then we'll stop and take on some water.' Easy.

When we stopped he told me that in about an hour we'd reach a beautiful view of the valley. And it was, indeed, wonderful. We rested for a few minutes. Then he told me about a tree, a further hour away up the hill, that we'd find full of birds. We got going again, it was tiring (well, for me), but the tree with the birds and the pretty birdsong was as promised.

The next stop, said my guide, would come after another hour of hard walking, and we'd stop for some lunch at the home of a Nepalese family. The lady of the house was welcoming, the food a delicious dhal, and we set off again refreshed, eagerly looking forward to the next stop at a bench up in the hills with my first view of the mountains.

By now, thanks to my lack of preparation, I was pretty tired. My legs hurt. But the promise of a glimpse of Annapurna gave me energy, and we got to the bench, me soaked in sweat, desperate for water and rest – and there we did indeed come upon the hint of a view – a sneak peak of our hazy goal.

Each section of our climb through the rich green forest brought a different thing to aim for. A view over paddy fields was spectacular, a stop for hot, green tea in a breezy hut extremely welcome. Finally my guide told me there was one more view to take in, at dusk, that was worth a little more pain and effort. We rounded a corner and ahead the sun was already low, illuminating the hills across from the one we'd been climbing. Time for one final push. It was getting dark, and all I could think of was the desperately needed hill lodge at the end. Where I eventually collapsed in a heap; relieved, broken, but there.

The next morning I was woken by my guide and invited onto the terrace for breakfast. Aching all over, I opened the door to reveal a perfectly flat lawn, with a huge, laden breakfast table surrounded by smiling people. And one of the world's most spectacular vistas: Annapurna South and Fishtail Mountain. It was the most breathtaking sight I had ever seen. And despite my lamentable lack of fitness, my wonderful guide had got me to the top to see it.

He'd done it step by step, in easily manageable increments, each with a motivating goal in mind. If he'd had started the day by saying, 'You're going to walk uphill for seven hours and the view from the top is amazing', I would have been less than enthusiastic, to say the least. If he had told me I'd have to climb up several thousand steep, broad stairs I wouldn't have started out at all. And if we had simply set off, I might have given up when my legs did.

But that well-practised guide knew exactly how to get me up that hill. Exactly how to make it all worthwhile. And somehow, though I knew I couldn't have got there on my own, the journey was fun, and I was proud to have made it.

This adventure – merely the first day of a truly wonderful month – impressed upon me the value of breaking down a journey for the people you're leading into a series of readily achievable goals.

In your business, you're that guide. It is up to you to get your team to the top. But first you have to make sure your team actually want to come with you. They need to know what you are aiming for. They need to see the lofty goal, so they can orient themselves correctly and muster the effort that will be needed. Then it's up to you to provide the motivation and temper the pace.

Your goal needs to be close enough to be desirable, and distant enough not to be intimidating. Your three-year goal might be a sale. Or to increase your current profit tenfold. Or both.

Perspective tells us that big things far away appear the same size as small things up close. So you need a big, simple, clear goal set near the horizon. And then, in focus in the foreground, you need granular and achievable steps that, when taken in the right order, will get you there.

This book is about how to turn this simple observation into a clear plan that will generate enthusiastic alignment and grow your business exceptionally rapidly. It doesn't matter when you put this framework and its processes in place. It has been employed equally effectively by twenty-year-old businesses, turnarounds, those that have stalled and startups.

Most entrepreneurial leaders try to do things too fast. Transformation implies speed. But rushing to implement change is a trap you probably recognise. You read a book or attend an event and learn something revolutionary. The next day you bring the new idea back to work and immediately put it into practice. After a few of these 'change grenades', staff begin to recognise the signs, and there is an upsurge of subtle eye-rolling and protective behaviours. Often new things don't get implemented at all, because the team knows there'll be another idea along next week.

So while a goal three years away must be bold and clear, the steps to get there must be precisely paced and specifically arranged so they can be undertaken by everyone in your team, one step at a time.

Big goal, small steps. Annapurna South; a valley, songbirds and hot, green tea.

The framework you will discover in this book makes turnaround or stellar growth easily achievable by you and your senior team. The mechanism is simple: break a long-term task into lots of easy little ones. It's the way this is done that makes this framework so supremely powerful.

The next few chapters will show you how the process works and how to implement it; what comes first, second and third; and how to bake it into your company's way of working. Subsequent chapters will deal with some of the critical growth enablers, including competitive differentiation and positioning, hiring and incentivising superstars, attracting new clients and compelling methods for pitching and winning clients.

Let's go.

Breaking through the levels

Some of the companies I've worked with had hit a bit of a plateau before they started the programme. You may have done so yourself. A lot of companies grow really fast, then reach some kind of invisible limit beyond which it seems impossible to go. This is usually accompanied by a fluctuating period of a bit up, a bit down: sometimes great, sometimes disheartening – and always frustrating. One of the problems with this kind of situation is that occasionally the wobbling up and down becomes more like a rollercoaster ride or, worse, a violent sea with tumultuous waves . . . you get the picture. And even without such instability pulling the leader's attention from one thing to another, external forces can quickly lead to capsize.

Most companies founded and run by entrepreneurs go through a couple of very predictable growth spurts, each of which ends in a flat period where no real growth happens. The first stage is usually zero to a million in revenue. This is where you gather around you a dozen or so people to help you build your dream. During this stage you'll prove that you have a product that has some market fit, and can find customers and sell it to them. The magic number in a team seems to be twelve people, where everyone does a bit of everything, you can all stand in for one another, the communication is great and you can all read each other's minds, and if you need to pull an all-nighter or two then beer and pizza is a ready cure. Then you hit your first ceiling. How do you expand from here?

This frustrating inability to make progress is the first time most entrepreneurs really have to think about how they grow, rather than what they sell. It's when you decide who you want to be working with for the foreseeable future – it's at this point I sometimes see one of the co-founders leave, because they find they're not quite where they want to be.

This is also when you realise you need a bookkeeper, or at least some kind of credit controller, and maybe someone to do organisational stuff like running the office. It can be a real drag getting past this phase, and you are likely to find yourself reaching out to a mentor with some similar experience to help you through it. Normally the solution is to learn how to run a business, by reading books like *Good to Great* by Jim Collins and asking your peers for advice on where to find more experienced staff. At the same time money gets tighter, because suddenly you're recruiting account handlers to manage your customers rather than just doing it yourself. Sometimes the resentment of having to pay someone else twice what you are paying yourself gets to you. We've all been there. But without addressing it successfully you won't break through.

Once you have, though, you'll find you're motoring again. Your newly acquired expertise alone (both personally and, now you've hired people with experience, as a business) will enable you to grow fast. And this will get you to just over a couple of million in annual revenue. By now you'll have a team of about twenty-four people – two lots of twelve again, but, rather than a single, happy family, there'll be an inner circle and an outer ring.

And then you level out again on the next plateau.

So far, then, you've got to your first million through dogged determination and the ability to sell what you supply, and your second by applying your brains and recruiting some talent.

To get beyond this new plateau you need to build in the scaffolding outlined in this book. It will take hard work and several months' dedicated application at the outset by a team that wants to become brilliant. Once you have the scaffolding in place, however, you can (to mix the metaphors) grease the poles, fill the balloon with helium, and your company will take off.

In reality, what you're doing by putting such a programme in place is breaking the two-year process into three phases: preparation (recruiting the team, laying the groundwork, getting staff used to change); building the machine (creating new processes that will allow scalability); and scaling (enacting the new policies and using them to minimise waste and maximise growth).

Any plan is always better than no plan

I ran startups for fifteen years before anyone told me that there were formulas you could use to make businesses work. What I observed during that time, both from talking to other founders and seeing what was happening in my own businesses, was that most entrepreneurs set a few goals at the beginning of each year and have a few big things they want to achieve. Then they set about achieving them. It's kind of haphazard, and always subject to the ups and downs of the sector you're working in.

For example, one year I had a plan to make our company famous (thereby attracting clients) by becoming the world's most awarded in its field. Not a bad goal, you might say. But it was effectively the only goal. And what was actually happening was that we were being buffeted from all sides – we'd recently sold the company on a three-year earnout, and I was having to rush around trying to understand and then control a P&L for the first time. Sometimes we had eight pitches on, sometimes none. One of my most senior people left and I needed to hire a replacement. A particular client got upset with us and we had to scramble to rebuild both the product and their trust. All this meant I was trying to enter (and then win) awards to make us famous in the midst of totally unpredictable chaos.

I did it, eventually. By the end of the year we were the world's most awarded digital agency.[1] I achieved, in that year, exactly one (profile-raising) thing – but there was no systematic improvement and it did nothing to help the company's transition to its new owners.

Most founders and leaders approach business this way: have a few goals for the year and hope you achieve them, and if you manage the most important two, that's a result.

Eventually I started working with the tools in this book and over many years refined them, standardised them, put them into practice in one company after another and proved they worked over and over again. Then I came to a startling realisation. It's one that might even cause you to stop reading this book right here. It's this:

Any plan is better than no plan.

It is not good enough just to have vision. It is not good enough just to have goals. (At best you'll achieve three or four goals a year.) It is not good enough to just have a guiding principle. You must have a plan of action.

Action.

[1] https://en.wikipedia.org/wiki/Head_New_Media

7

A plan of action consists of a series of defined deliverables, an order of events, and a schedule.

Then you have to stick to it.

It is almost infinitely easier when you have a team around you to help you. So you should really share out the responsibility for delivering the plan. Even better is to get someone external in to guide you through the execution of the plan on time and in the right order. A top-quality advisor should teach you most of the things you'll need to learn, change or upgrade. They will help you develop your team and, perhaps more importantly, hold you to account.

And that's where this book comes in. While any plan is better than no plan, the right plan is better than any plan. If you follow this book's approach to developing your plan and executing it you can expect to at least double or triple your turnover in two years. This book is all about this framework, 2Y3X®.

KEY TAKEAWAYS

- Most businesses go through growth stages. Each stage takes effort and requires new methods, systems and processes.
- Any plan is better than no plan. Any plan you execute is better than the best plan in the world that's not implemented.
- Big change is best approached in little steps; breaking a grand plan down into easily managed stages means it is more easily – and much more likely to be – carried out.
- All diagrams and illustrations in this book can be downloaded from https://scaleatspeed.com/illustrations/

1

Strategic Goals

Strategy versus planning

Why does this book focus on developing a plan of action, rather than developing strategy?

Strategy is such an over-used word. I ran a strategy consultancy. I misused the word frequently to make clients feel important. Now it just irritates me when people confuse strategy (a general plan) with tactics (its specific actions). This book is about how to achieve strategic goals using a practical framework for all the tactical changes you will need to implement to achieve them. This book is, in fact, not about strategy but how to implement strategy.

Your goal may, for example, be to sell your company at the highest possible price. You will need to understand both the strategic context (when will prices be highest?) and the tactical requirements (what will make a buyer pay the highest price?). The Strategy Map you will unfurl in this book starts with the strategic goals and works backwards to define the prerequisites and necessary tactics to deliver them. The 2Y3X Roadmap outlines this strategically useful series of tactical activities and puts them in order.

In the United Kingdom the business cycle usually lasts around sixty-two months from peak to peak, with a standard error of twenty-eight months[2] (in the United States the cycle is sixty-nine months[3]). That's a little over five years. So if you want to sell your business, and the acquirer wants to pay you over an earn-out period of three years

[2] http://www.econ.cam.ac.uk/research-files/repec/cam/pdf/wp0024.pdf
[3] https://www.investopedia.com/ask/answers/071315/what-average-length-boom-and-bust-cycle-us-economy.asp

based on your achieving increasing financial goals, then to maximise what you will get you'll need to time the deal exactly right. If the deal is done at a multiple of the average profit over the three years of an earn-out, then in an ideal world you will sell three years before the next business cycle peak, in order to realise the maximum possible value – assuming your business follows the business cycle in terms of its optimum growth.

Similarly, if you're in a business with a limited shelf life (let's say retouching photographs by hand, a craft likely to be replaced by AI, or tuning car engines, with petrol cars set to be superseded by electric cars), then this should be taken into consideration. You may either wish to exit before your business becomes redundant, or build in a step-by-step plan to move from one specialisation to the next.

Other strategic considerations include climate change affecting population movement or market demand; trends that affect whether consumers go out to socialise or stay in but use social media; population growth or shrinkage; shifts in the acceptability of things like foreign tourism and environmental impact; changes in the supply of raw materials or talent; or politics.

Businesses need to consider all of these, increasingly so the further the horizon their leaders set for themselves. The long view means that surprises will be fewer and farther between.

The SWOT

A SWOT (Strengths, Weaknesses, Opportunities, Threats) table can help to focus your thinking. If you haven't done one recently I would recommend you do, and update it as often as possible, as it will influence some of the decisions you'll be making during the 2Y3X process. In my experience your SWOT need only contain four or five items per section. This focuses your team on those that will or could have the greatest impact. By concentrating on the most important things, it should be easy for you to identify anything that poses an existential threat.

Strengths – Internal	Weaknesses – Internal
Clear internal communication	Cashflow
Highly efficient processes	Some disengaged staff
Total alignment of purpose	No training
Great marketing team	Biggest customer is 40% of revenue
	Not profitable enough
Opportunities – External	**Threats – External**
Attracting other big clients	Competitors moving into our niche
Switzerland	Poaching of staff
Profitable add-on services	Biggest customer leaves
Focus on niche market leadership	Change of government
	Forex

A sample SWOT for a consulting firm

Looking at the example above, if your biggest client – accounting for 40 per cent of your company's revenue – were to give notice and leave, then you would have an enormous amount of work to do in order to survive. You would have to scale down salaries as fast as possible to match the reduced income, rebalance the remaining team and maintain morale. You would also have to maintain market position in the face of competitors moving into your niche and poaching your worried staff. This critical weakness ought to have a chilling effect, and force you to confront the issue head-on and immediately.

What should you do? Well, your options boil down to reducing the amount of exposure to a single client by: reducing your work for them; upscaling other clients; or winning additional big clients. Sales and client services will find themselves working hard.

By contrast, the opportunity in Switzerland is low priority and should be deferred until the crisis has been averted, or delegated to someone otherwise unoccupied.

Of use here is the quadrant diagram[4] *Urgent vs. Important* articulated by Stephen Covey in *The Seven Habits of Highly Effective People,* which provides a ready reckoner of what is important enough for you, the leader, to focus on now or in the future, and what could be delegated to others. The standard joke is that this diagram is the easiest tool for getting rid of half your workload. However, it also requires that

How to halve your workload.

---

[4] I've always been told that quadrant diagrams are silly, but this one has always struck me as being particularly useful. The problem with it, of course, is that you have to remember to add it to your schedule to do it every now and again.

you learn how to delegate. By the end of this book you will hopefully be so enthused by the 2Y3X Roadmap process that you'll want to hand off to others almost everything you now spend your day doing so you can get out of the weeds and into the strategy-o-sphere. There is a section on delegation in Chapter 2.

Another perspective on this came from a colleague who ran one of the departments in a company I co-founded and of which I was CEO and rainmaker-in-chief.

I used to think that PR (public relations) was the most important thing for me to do. I spent a lot of time talking to journalists, writing articles, appearing on stages and developing activities that would get us noticed in the press and our industry. It was, it must be said, both enjoyable and extremely effective: it generated almost all our inbound leads and over the years translated into millions in sales.

However, as CEO I was also the main salesperson in the company. It was me leading the pitches the PR generated. One day I was the subject of an intervention. I was sat down and it was pointed out to me in no uncertain terms that I was being foolish doing all that PR. 'But...' – and I countered with all the above.

Then I was shown the maths. I spent 30 per cent of my time on PR. And 30 per cent on selling. Yet any PR expert could do what I was doing on PR; no-one, however, could sell the company's services (at the time) as well as I could. If I delegated the PR, in other words, I would *double the time I could spend on selling*.

I let that sink in. Then I stopped doing stuff other people could do, often better than me, and my company became successful.

First, the end

'The journey of a thousand miles', Lao Tsu famously wrote, 'starts with a single step.'

Steve Jobs famously said, 'It is impossible to see how the dots join up except in retrospect.'

In life we tend to set out on adventures knowing that we don't know where they will lead, and that it may be more of an accidental journey than one that comes out as planned. In business, however, you are entering into a transaction with your future self. You do not go into business to fail, but to succeed. You have a vision, no matter how vague, and you want to see it come to life. You have goals, and you want to see them achieved.

It is possible to use hindsight to inform future plans. In fact, it would be entirely prudent to do so. For some reason, as entrepreneurs in business, it is very rare that we seek out experienced hands to guide this journey, despite the fact that most businesses make exactly the same mistakes as their predecessors, and fail for exactly the same reasons. At the very least it is surely wise to avoid the mistakes that plague businesses the world over, and learn as much as you can about which shortcuts work, so you may apply them. This lessens the risk of not achieving your goals, or having your journey cut short through business failure.

By applying others' hindsight you can create processes that steady the company so it can grow, accelerate excellence, drive profits and in due course liberate you from those very processes to exercise your creativity and imagination so you can better meet the future.

The simplest way of looking at the steps you'll need to take is to understand what sort of journey you want to go on. You need to have a rough idea of what you want to happen. Even if it's not an end goal, but only an intermediate step. Like my climb – just the first day of a month in Nepal – it needs to be articulated so that you can align your plans and your team.

A three-year horizon is useful. It is long enough that you can get several things done between now and then, and short enough that you can keep it constantly in mind. From a practical point of view, it is also short enough that the goalposts are likely to be in roughly the same place when you get there, and if they do shift, you can readily adapt.

The first action, therefore, is to set a three-year target.

Once you have done this, you work backwards to define the elements that will be required to get there, starting with those activities closest to achieving the goal, and ending with those closest to where you are now.

I have therefore structured the book in the same way as the programme is structured. In fact, it is exactly the same as the approach taken by my Nepalese guide. It's all based on standing at the top of the mountain and looking back down the path to work out the waypoints. In practice, we look back at those waypoints and tweak them constantly, optimising the order, their placement, their scale, frequency and amplitude.

This is how this 2Y3X programme has been devised, revised, taught and implemented. It is the result of constant iteration, but always starts with an eagle's-eye view from the top of the hill at the end of the trail. This end point is a tiny collection of lofty goals. These goals are where you want to be in three years' time. They will include a financial component, a culture component and a product standards component. For the sake of illustration these might be:

- £2 million net profit (EBIT)[5]
- *The Times*'s Top 100 Employers list (TT100)
- Company of the Year

Next we work out what needs to be in place to meet these goals. For example, in order to be making £2 million EBIT, if your ideal net profit level is 20 per cent then your gross profit needs to be £10 million, for which you're likely – depending on your industry's norms – to need a hundred staff (at £100K gross profit per head), and of course you need to be reaching your 20 per cent net profit mark consistently. Each of

---

[5] Earnings Before Interest and Tax (EBIT) or Operating Profit.

these requirements may in turn require major change from where you are today, and therefore we break the difference down into a series of stepped actions. For simplicity and clarity, we divide these actions into five broad subject areas:

1. People
2. Customers/clients
3. Sales and marketing
4. Processes
5. Corporate and financial

So, having unpacked the three-year goals into a list of things that need to be true in the third year in order for the goals to be attained, we need to reverse-engineer the process of arriving at the final destination.

Let's take one component: a hundred staff on the books. If today you have thirty staff then you need to treble your headcount and some. With a hundred staff you will need a middle-management team running the show, and a senior team will have had to identify, recruit and train that middle tier. Do you have a senior team yet? Are they trained? Do they have a plan?

These activities necessarily fall out of the need for a hundred staff:

- ✓ One hundred staff
- ✓ Middle-management layer
- ✓ Management training
- ✓ Identify middle managers
- ✓ Growth strategy
- ✓ Assemble the growth team

There is a clear (top-down) linear path to reaching your goal of employing your hundred people. But have you forgotten your other goal of being in the *Times* Top 100 Employers list? This affects everything:

- ✓ One hundred *highly motivated* staff
- ✓ *Exceptional* middle-management layer *plus* internal TT100 programme
- ✓ Management training *plus* staff training *plus* staff incentives
- ✓ Growth strategy *plus* employee engagement plan
- ✓ Growth team assembled

Now this is richer and more rounded. It requires a holistic approach. It may even deliver much of what's required to make your company 'Company of the Year' too. Though you'll need to add in a PR programme, a process to look after awards, a process to look after quality control, client satisfaction . . .

The beauty of the 2Y3X system is that from some very simple but lofty goals, an awful lot of required situations and actions will emerge. It can feel complex, and in truth it is highly complex, but by breaking everything down into small actions you can assign these actions to people as tasks, and by approaching them judiciously you can make it all feel – to the people delivering this flowering garden – simple.

For sanity's sake we break all the actions down into periods. The easiest to manage are years, quarters and months. Your three-year goals become three individual years, each broken down into four quarterly tasks. Each of these three-month periods is in turn broken down into month 1, *research*; month 2, *prototype/draft/test*; month 3 is *roll-out*.

This gives you the capacity over the course of three years to deliver twelve change-enabling actions. If you have a team of five people working on these strategically important tasks, then that's sixty change-effecting projects that will be delivered over three years. And yet, each person will only ever be doing one thing at a time. This is why the 2Y3X system actually works. It's because it feels like it's *easy*. In fact, it's so efficient that after a couple of years you will have made almost all the changes required to reach your three-year goal. The reason 2Y3X is so named is that it's a two-year programme that delivers a three-year goal of tripling revenue.

In practice, although the three lofty goals you've set look as though they might imply twenty actions, the reality is that you have to do plenty of groundwork in order to create a scalable company. Many of the things in this book will seem like common sense, and some of them you will already have in place. But getting all of them in place, in the right order, and dovetailing them together into a lattice, is what will enable your company to grow. And once you've done all the groundwork, made all of the basic changes and put in place all the required stakes and poles and netting, your company will accelerate at such a fast pace you won't even recognise it.

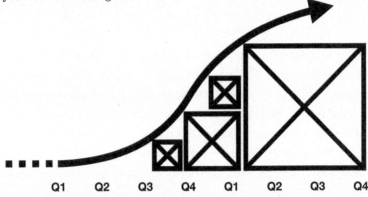

| Q1 | Q2 | Q3 | Q4 | Q1 | Q2 | Q3 | Q4 |

Once the building blocks are in place you will start
to see your growth accelerate.

The Strategy Map

Let's now look at how the Strategy Map is generated.

First, a few acknowledgements. The Strategy Map builds on principles outlined in Robert Kaplan and David Norton's book *Balanced Scorecard* and the subsequent tools developed by CapGemini to deliver large-scale technology transformation projects. The 2Y3X Roadmap (though without a strategic context tool) is partly based on *Execution Maximiser*,[6] developed by Jim Alampi, which itself is based on Verne Harnish's superb book *Scaling Up*.

Scaling Up is a stunning business manual. However, implementing it requires significant resources – and it is extraordinarily complex. To understand, implement and cascade all of its processes and tools is out of the reach of most small or medium-sized businesses, and the ongoing management of most of its tools is resource-intensive. The book you have in front of you, on the other hand, is based on twenty-five years of using various frameworks while whittling them down to something simple enough to be practical. It dispenses with distractions and nice-to-haves like purpose, vision, mission, brand promise, etc. – these are all great, but only when you've got nothing else to sort out and your growth is already 40 per cent plus per year.

The 2Y3X Roadmap is therefore a tool derived from several sources, and simplified so as to be easily manageable by a small senior team and applied specifically to drive very rapid growth. Its content is drawn from the Strategy Map you will learn how to build.

In order, the stages of implementation are:

- Goal setting
- Growth team creation
- Identification of values and the unifying proposition
- Strategy Map development
- 2Y3X Roadmap development
- Trial quarter

The Strategy Map is fairly straightforward. It looks like the diagram on the following page.

[6] All product names, trademarks and registered trademarks are property of their respective owners. All company, product and service names used in this book are for identification purposes only.

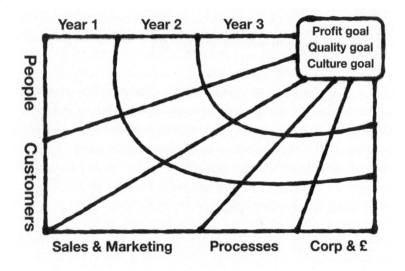

The Strategy Map

As you can see, in the top-right-hand corner are listed the targets. The chart is then broken down into three concentric annual sections. It is then split into five radial sections: People; Customers; Sales and Marketing; Processes; Corporate and Financial.

The radial sections represent the critical attention areas of the business. As you will have noticed, there isn't a section for Product. In this method we assume that product is a function (in both senses of the word) of the way the business is managed. In other words, if product quality has an effect on customer retention or market positioning then any activity related to product refinement or improvement should be included in those sections. Likewise, innovation planning should be included in Processes, investment in equipment in Financial, and so on. This allows the 2Y3X Roadmap process to be about the business, not about the product – and businesses can be fixed, improved and grown fast, no matter what they do, provided there is management alignment and whole-company focus on what needs to be done now and next.

Each radial section is worked backwards from the targets. This means that, for example, where one goal is to be ready for sale, in the People section in Year 3 that year's activities might include *Senior Management Team (SMT) running the business; MD in place*. The year prior to that, the activities might include *Select SMT members for promotion to board* and *Identify two MD candidates in team plus one external candidate*. In the final year, i.e. next year looking from today, *Permanent SMT identified; training programme in place*.

To deliver the tasks for the coming year you will need to select several SMT candidates, identify what training will be required, and eventually establish some kind of incentive programme for them.

Working backwards from the SMT (or GLT – see Chapter 2) being in charge in Year 3, in Year 1 you will identify them and in Year 2 allow them time to practise on the job.

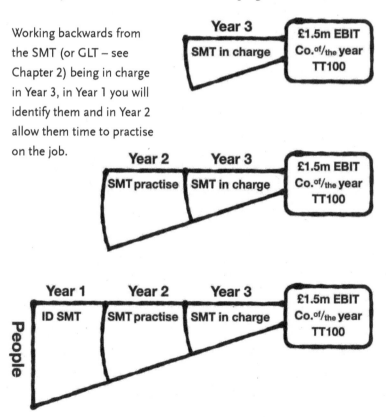

Within the same People section will be some additional requirements. These are based on an external view of what needs improving in the business – for instance, hiring a new cadre of A-player recruits as the company expands. Again, this implies a formal hiring strategy, an HR process (which goes into the Process section), a people-development programme, Job Scorecard and KPI setting, and so on.

Remember: you are starting at the end, looking at the state the company needs to be in in order that the goals are achieved at the end of the third year. What will you have in place? Only once you have established this should you move back one year to Year 2 to look at what will need to be going on then, and what you'll need to have in place for Year 3 to be possible.

As you can see, this process flowers, and the closer we get to today the more there are specifically defined tasks to be done. This is normal. Usually there will end up being between sixteen and twenty tasks to be completed in Year 1, spread across all the segments. These will take us up to the start of Year 2, when a new set of activities will be called for, leading to Year 3 when you are preparing to meet the goals.

This process is fractal. While some activities may appear fairly broad, they can be broken down into smaller tasks. This provides the opportunity to apply the same principle of task identification to more junior staff or departments – delegating a few small tasks which add up to the delivery of a top-level quarterly initiative.

This, then, is the Strategy Map. Its output is the tasks, actions and changes you need to make this coming year, allocated to a team you need to build. This task list will be prioritised.

Opposite: The progression of the Strategy Map as you work backwards, with some example tasks.

(ERP is an Enterprise Resource Platform like Oracle or SAP; CSS is Customer Satisfaction Score; NPD is New Product Development; GP is Gross Profit.)

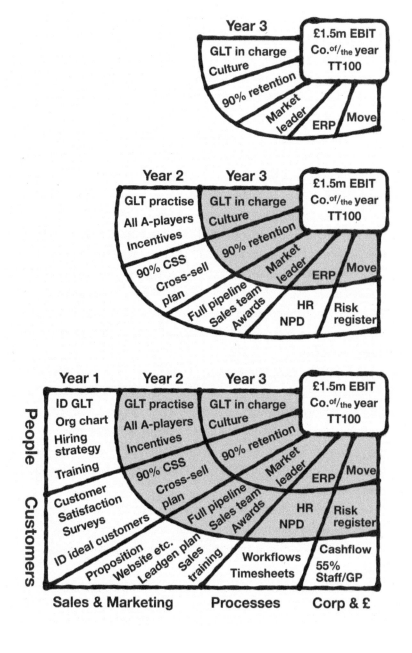

I've worked with owners and leadership teams in marketing consultancies, ad agencies, staffing firms, back-end developers, private equity firms, holding groups, Machine Learning companies and tech startups. Over numerous implementations of the Strategy Map process, many of the same issues come up repeatedly, no matter what sector the firm operates in.

Something I learned while I was a member of Vistage, a 23,000-member CEO-mentoring organisation, was that all businesses have the same growing pains. My own observation from running half a dozen of my own companies and chairing more than a dozen more is that it doesn't really matter what scale you are at now: if you want to make the next step of increasing your size and value, then you'll need to address similar issues at the beginning of each period of accelerated growth.

Some of these issues will become obvious once you have worked through the Strategy Map. The rest of this book will look at how that's done, and lay out some more or less universally applicable and useful tools that will make your life easier as you go through the process of transformation.

As a structure, the Strategy Map is formidable. With solid chairing of regular monthly progress meetings, you will find that progress, when relentlessly pursued, delivers huge changes within even the first six months, and that this pace of change increases rapidly, even if it may seem slow at first. The 2Y3X Programme, which uses this framework, routinely doubles the revenue of the companies that participate in it.

Now we've established the frameworks that create the armature for accelerating growth, we need to pin down the focal point for the company, before diving into each key focus area covered by the Strategy Map.

But first we need to start at the very end, by setting and defining your goals.

BHAG

The author of *Good to Great*, Jim Collins, believes that every company needs to set itself a truly epic and ambitious goal in order to frame its mission. He calls this the BHAG: big, hairy, audacious goal. I love this. It forces you to do several things:

- Imagine a staggeringly successful future where you've achieved the pinnacle of your potential.
- Imagine a better world that is the result of the work you have done.
- Think really big, rather than incrementally.

To use some well-known examples, Amazon's was, 'Every book ever printed in any language in your hands in less than 60 seconds'; Microsoft's: 'A computer on every desk and in every home'.

They're common knowledge now. Because they were so ambitious and so outrageous when they were articulated, and yet they came true. Why? Because they were articulated. Had they not been, people would have been looking to achieve lesser things and none of the above would have happened. It takes vision to create a mission. It takes foresight and crazy ambition. If you have a vision it makes it easy to convey to your partners, customers, employees, family. Without it there's nothing to believe in. 'I believe in you, daughter,' is nowhere near as powerful as 'I believe in your vision, daughter' – the latter is something that can propagate, and propagation through the group of people who will turn it into reality is essential if there is to be focus and coherence and dedication to a plan that will enable you all to reach the goal.

The BHAG was defined as being a ten-to-thirty-year goal, with a clear success metric so you know when it has been achieved. This is inspiring and absolutely correct when thinking about the life of a company in the long term. It's the framing device for what you do as a corporation. However, for our purposes this timeframe is less practical. We're looking for a three-year goal set.

The idea of something lofty, though, is perfect for us.

When I ran my own companies, at least in the early days, it was common for us to fly blind and just let the businesses live without any growth goals. My first two companies were there to change the world, but as we forgot to set any financial goals, although they shone brightly and played their part in the digital revolution, neither was financially successful.

Over the past quarter-century I've worked with many, many companies who initially view growth as an incremental exercise. They start from where they are now, rather than from the viewpoint of where they want to be. Incremental growth of, say, 10–15 per cent year on year has the unfortunate effect of making flat revenue or even shrinkage fall within the margin for error. The result is that reaching a particular financial target means the goal line moves by years rather than by amount. Neither flying blind nor incremental goal-setting leads reliably to rapid growth or financial success.

Setting a three-year goal by ignoring where you are today and focusing rather on where you'd like to be in an ideal world gives so much more scope to fire up your imagination and be big, hairy and audacious in your ambition. The bigger and more incredible it is the better, in my experience. Why? Because it will force you to come up with a vision.

With a truly ambitious goal you may be forced to think laterally. Setting your profit at ten times its current level means you can't just do business as usual, make cost savings or increase your prices by 10 per cent. You may have to raise some capital and buy three or four other businesses. If you did that, what would they have to look like? How would you have to prepare? What new skills would you have to learn? What skills would you have to hire in? Suddenly you're in a whole new ball game.

How about having a goal of being the top-rated employer in your country? That's not just about giving people bananas on Tuesdays.

For those who are scared by visionary thinking, there's another more practical reason to set a hefty target: we tend to just miss targets. I was working with an agency that went on to win five company-of-the-year awards in its industry. When we started they were coming up to their financial year end. The owner and I were discussing targets. I asked what they'd set the previous year. £2.4 million in revenue, he said. And how's it going? 'Nearly there, a bit short, but I've put up an incentive plan.' By the year end they'd missed the target by just £400.

Even more common is missing your goal by 10 per cent. If you set a £2.4 million target and missed by 10 per cent you'd make £2.16 million. Not bad at all, you might think. But if you'd done £2.18 million the previous year and had set the target at £2.4 million, then missed your target by 10 per cent, you'd have made less this year than you made last year (£2.16 million).

By setting a target that's radically higher, we're removing the possibility that a near miss actually means a year-on-year decrease in revenue.

By setting a target of double the revenue, a 10 per cent miss means you've still increased revenue by 80 per cent.

And there's a psychological effect at play here too. We tend to think that big numbers are less achievable than little numbers. If people are put off by big goals, they can be broken down into smaller, more achievable-sounding goals. I'm no mathematician, but I do know that doubling your revenue in two years sounds much tougher than adding 3 per cent revenue each month – which delivers the 100 per cent increase in two years. Or doubling revenue in two years only requires 40 per cent a year. Spread over three years it requires just 26 per cent a year. Easy!

The companies I work with are usually set a challenging target of tripling revenue in three years. It forces them to think differently about the changes they will need to make in order to become a well-run company of a very different size.

Goal-setting theory

As an entrepreneur you already know that the tougher the challenge, the more likely it is that you will succeed at it. Edwin Locke is a psychologist who has made a career of studying the effects of setting different kinds of challenges, and how the way those challenges are described, ordered and managed affects the outcome. In 1968 Locke wrote a treatise called 'Toward a theory of task motivation and incentives', and his work on goal-setting theory (GST) has been validated repeatedly.

Locke essentially says that:

- The harder the goal, the higher the performance.
- A specific goal performs better than a vague goal.

A later study also by Locke showed that 90 per cent of challenges set according to these rules outperformed non-challenging or non-specific goals.

The other thing that's really interesting is that goal-setting performance is also related to the proximity of the goal.[7] The division of a big goal into smaller goals with a shorter delivery deadline means the appearance of diminishing returns is less likely. Set a target too far away, and at some point the immediate pressure wears off and the returns appear to fade. In other words, there's no point in setting a really hard goal far away without setting some hard intermediate goals along the way. Just setting me a 6,000-stair climb would never have got me to the top in Nepal. It required a series of intermediate steps.

So you need to set goals that are hard and specific, that are near enough to the present that the challenge won't dissipate the longer they go on, and which add up to the main long-term goals.

Locke and fellow psychologist Gary Latham also described how feedback is important to the process. This feedback needs to be

[7] Steel and Konig, *Temporal Motivation Theory* (2006).

external, and related to your performance on each task. This, for me, is the compelling reason for having an external advisor guiding the 2Y3X Programme. You need someone from the outside validating your work, teaching you where you don't know the answers, and encouraging you to reach challenging goals by reassuring you that you can do it.

GST in fact proposes an order in which tasks should be set. Learning goals must come before implementation goals. So the 2Y3X Roadmap works on the basis of first doing the groundwork, gathering data and doing research, before prototyping and implementing new processes. In turn, the new processes add up to broader capabilities, and ultimately the three-year goal is greater than the sum of its parts. It works because it starts with smaller, more easily achievable tasks, building confidence and capability, before going on to complex, whole-business tasks.

So here are the rules:[8]

- Make your goal difficult (yet attainable).
- Be specific.
- Combine long- and short-term goals.
- Be committed.
- Set learning goals before outcome goals.

This feeds into one final point from GST: that the higher someone's self-efficacy (their belief they can complete a task), the more likely they are to set a task that challenges them. The team you assemble, therefore, needs to be managed correctly: learning before doing, feedback based on performance, and confidence building over time. You will find after six or nine months that your team is becoming exceptionally effective. The team's selection is therefore going to be crucial in shaping your business in the future.

[8] Mark Koester, *Towards a Science of Goals: Goal Setting as a Key Influence on Performance*: http://www.markwk.com/science-of-goals.html

Setting long-term targets

Most people in a stable business, when asked what their growth target is for the coming year, will come up with a 'reasonable' number. This is usually something like 10 or 20 per cent growth. We all like to set goals that we believe we can easily reach.

Yet if we miss the goal by ten percentage points, we've only grown a very small amount. This lays us open to market fluctuations and unexpected crises like a big client moving to a different supplier, a senior member of staff joining a more exciting competitor, or even illness. The consequence is stagnation, lurching between feast and famine, and stress. We are unable to build cash reserves and profits to fuel growth, and ultimately even the committed entrepreneur will get bored and lose focus after very few years. The one thing the entrepreneur needs for continued motivation is success, and lack of growth feels like failure. It's the same for their staff. Long-timers tend to be at best B-players, at worst C-players. Lack of ambition and dynamic enthusiasm is reflected in how potential customers see the company, and the end result is slow decline and 'For sale as a going concern' on retirement.

On the other hand, if we set an aggressive goal over too short a timeframe it may feel implausible. Doubling gross profit (GP) in a year would be likely to require very significant investment. And with the best will in the world, if we invest in new salespeople, project managers, production staff or facilities, it will take a couple of months to find them and a few more months before they are up to speed and producing revenue. There is no point in setting yourself up for failure, so most people who are focusing on the coming year's targets will naturally avoid that.

So how do we set targets that are 'unreasonable' yet achievable?

To resolve the implied contradiction you can turn to the principle of compound interest. Imagine you want to double your gross profit in two years. (Using a gross profit target for now allows you to set aside the fact that you may not yet be making a most desirable 20 per cent net profit.[9]) On the face of it, doubling in two years is an ambitious target, and one that most will balk at. However, by looking at this from the perspective of taking just one little (monthly 3 per cent) step at a time, compound interest makes it much more palatable.

My experience is that a three-year target is useful, because it allows time for onboarding a new strategy and spinning up the resources that will be required to achieve it. Only then can you accelerate.

Setting a target of three times gross profit in three years also requires 3 per cent growth per month. But at the end, even if you miss by thirty percentage points, you've doubled the gross profits of the company. And that gives you cash for growth as well as an appreciable achievement. Objectively, the entrepreneur has created success, and along the way has created more value for shareholders, greater stability for the company, and a more exciting environment for staff.

It doesn't really matter what the three-year target is if it achieves these effects. If you have a strong balance sheet of well over three times monthly costs (see the later chapter on essential KPIs), and strong cashflow to support it, then you might want to increase your target and invest in more aggressive growth through acquisition. For the sake of this book I will continue to use the 3x example as it has proved to be realistic, achievable using the methods outlined here, and sufficiently motivating.

So you now have a top-line target: three times gross profit in three years.

You also need an underlying target: net profit as a percentage of gross profit. In most of the businesses I work with this target is around 20 per cent. Any less and you risk having too little to both invest in growth and provide a buffer for unexpected emergencies or market

[9] Net profit is addressed later on; the goal in that regard is to set and maintain a net profit target of, say, 20 per cent, and there are a number of ways to do this.

changes. Any more and you are simply collecting cash and likely to be distributing it to shareholders without investing it in innovation – staying ahead of the competition and addressing future needs of customers – or reinvesting it in growth.

Reinvesting excess profits in driving additional growth will sharply increase the value of the company if you can sell it at a multiple of profits or revenue. The multiple of profits paid for a small business on sale rises the bigger the company gets, as scale is less risky. A larger company is likely to have strategies for risk reduction, many of which are covered in this book, and these are attractive to acquirers. So at half a million of net profit the price might be three times the average profit over three years; at a million net profit the price might be five times the average net profit over a three year earn-out. The difference is huge:

Average net profit over 3 years (£400K) x 4 (Multiple)

= £1.6 million

Average net profit over 3 years (£800K) x 6 (Multiple)

= £4.8 million

In other words, doubling your net profit would more than triple your sale value.

2x	EBIT	Multiple	Value
Year 1	400k	4	1.6m
Year 3	800k	6	4.8m
			3x

NB: In the US, multiples are lower due to the greater number of sellers.

3x	EBIT	Multiple	Value
Year 1	400k	4	1.6m
Year 3	1.2m	10	12m
			7.5x

Tripling your EBIT over three
years would multiply your value over seven times.

For this reason, the owners should take less in salary and contribute more to profit. In the long run they will make more money owing to the multiplier effect.

If you want to sell your business and hand it over to your senior team to run so you can leave at some point, your successors will want to be incentivised to stay with the company and grow it. Having correctly motivated people in place will add to your company's attractiveness to potential buyers. In that case you will probably want to grant shares or share options to your successors. Having a decent pie to share means you getting rewarded for the work you've put in founding and growing the company, and even if their portion of the pie is relatively small, the more it is worth the more meaningful an incentive it will be.

Quality and culture

What other targets should be included? It seems straightforward to set financial targets, but while they are useful for business planning, they aren't in themselves motivating to staff.

Time and again I have seen staff complaining that their firm has become too focused on the money, which in turn inevitably leads to questions about where the money is going. Many employees believe that profits are pocketed by the owners, and that their hard work is simply funding a lavish lifestyle for those at the top. This causes problems for managers – demands for raises or promotions when staff see profit targets being met, lack of motivation (not everyone is motivated by the promise of future money), or even a focus on short-term profits to meet targets at the expense of long-term growth, client satisfaction or product or service quality.

Pure profit focus also leads to tribalism and fracture within medium-sized or larger companies, with different departments each believing that their role is to drive profits without reference to the wider good of the company. For example, the finance department may demand reduction in supplier costs, which may mean supplier quality or productivity is reduced. This in turn creates stress in project management where timely delivery is reduced, and client satisfaction is eroded. Great people start looking for other jobs, increasing staff turnover and the HR team's associated recruitment and onboarding costs. And all because the finance department is trying to meet the company's profitability target.

So there needs to be a clear target that is motivating, challenging and unifying for all of the people in your business, not just the owners.

Whatever the solution is, it must intrinsically drive the financial results you require, without referencing financial targets directly. The great manager sets goals that encourage positive behaviours and integration with the rest of the company, rather than creating complicated and potentially divisive motivational strategies. A later chapter talks about how to set individual performance goals and measurement criteria, but for now you need to find a simple, quantifiable and motivating measure of success. And like all targets, goals and measures, whatever you choose must have a goal line: people need to be able to see that they are progressing towards it, and to know when they have reached it. If over three years you set an ambitious and motivating goal, and it is achieved, then you must find the next. Revisiting your strategy every year, and redesigning it for the much larger organisation that you will be after three years, is critical to continued focus and success.

Here are two examples that I have found to work:

1. **Customer satisfaction measured both internally and through industry recognition**

   Setting a three-year target of achieving a consistent 95 per cent average customer satisfaction score gives staff a clear goal to aim for. It encourages people to work together to find optimal ways to do it, and will inevitably improve client relationships. This leads to more repeat business, more referrals, higher revenues, lower sales costs, higher staff retention, and of course increased profits. Using the scores as the basis for industry recognition (PR, awards, referrals) attracts bigger and better clients, higher-calibre staff and potential acquirers.

   Some industry award schemes might also serve this purpose well. The UK's Drum Recommends Awards are based on independently gathered client satisfaction scores. Less direct but still perfectly viable are industry and peer-judged awards given to your own sector's best performing companies. A data company/food service provider/airline/recruitment firm/IT consultancy of the year award, won two or three years in a row, is a strong indicator that your firm is considered to be at or near the apex of its specialism.

2. **Staff motivation measured both internally and through industry recognition**

   One of the companies I worked with set a goal of joining the *Sunday Times* 100 Best Companies to Work For list. A committee was formed to understand what it would take to get there. They devised a plan for rolling out a programme of work that led to higher staff engagement, satisfaction and advocacy, while also being mindful of non-negotiable profit targets. There was a lot of work to be done, but by setting the target the staff knew their employer was committed to making their company an exceptional place to work. Greater staff engagement leads to higher levels of creativity and innovation, increased client satisfaction and retention, and (because great people actively attract other great people) lower recruitment costs. All of which also leads to higher profits.

For any business, setting goals for customer or client satisfaction would seem to be a no-brainer. And for any business that relies on its staff to attract and retain customers or recruit high-quality colleagues, setting an objective target for staff motivation would also seem sensible.

For the latter, however, just setting staff satisfaction scores as a target may encourage the wrong behaviours by managers. For example, it's easy to keep people happy by giving them time off, lots of holidays or rapid promotion (which will probably have unintended and unwelcome consequences). Such good intentions may actually be to the detriment of productivity, client satisfaction or profit. By tying the target to an objective set of standards like those required to make the *Sunday Times* 100 Best Companies to Work For league, you can be more sure of getting a balanced and collaborative approach to the task, rather than one which just serves an individual's immediate targets. Other metrics like Net Promoter Score (NPS) or GlassDoor reviews can also be extremely useful as measures, and setting ambitious targets like consistently exceeding 90 per cent can demand a focus on new and positive management behaviours.

As the leader of your company, you ultimately have the

responsibility to set a strategy that will align and unify. The 2Y3X Roadmap framework is essentially a blank template for achieving a set of targets. The best way to create coherence and cohesion is to get the team to collaborate in identifying and prioritising all the elements that will go into reaching them. This is a sure-fire way of creating real engagement at the top level of the company. And if you include a couple of more junior staff – potential superstars – in the team it will go a long way to making the whole company feel like it has a stake in its future.

KEY TAKEAWAYS

- Every business needs to know what its strategy is, given both the current and future market for its services. A SWOT is a great place to start identifying your priorities.
- Define your three-year goals at the start: this is far enough away to be aspirational, yet close enough to be within reach.
- Goal-setting theory has demonstrated that the more challenging the goal, the more likely a high-performing team is to achieve it.
- Set three targets: financial, quality and culture. These will balance each other and drive desirable behaviours as you progress towards your goals.

2

The 2Y3X Process

Building the growth lab team

The people you assemble to deliver the 2Y3X Roadmap will essentially constitute a Petri dish for the business's succession team. With practice they will eventually take over the running of your company. It should include people who may not be the immediate successors to your current leadership team, but belong to its next generation.

If one of the goals is for the owner to exit the business through trade sale, then it is imperative that succession is sorted out well in advance – any potential acquirer knows that there is a strong likelihood that the vendor will leave soon after the sale, and in any case once any earn-out is complete. In advance of this an identified team must be in place, either in training or in ready positions, and appropriately incentivised and of course forewarned. This new team is the ideal training ground in which responsibility can be learned alongside strategic planning and the collaborative delivery of transformative steps.

While this cohort is often made up of the senior managers in the business, you should bring more junior people into the team if they are potential superstars – or are more likely to get things done than other senior managers, who are often brilliant at managing teams but terrible at delivering strategically useful projects outside their area of expertise. Ultimately the team is responsible for growing the business by addressing important blockages, developing new processes, or building out new strategies.

When I started using the frameworks this book describes, it seemed natural to use the existing SMT as the team to plan and execute the changes the Roadmap describes. However, two clients showed me my error. One company that I chaired was fairly young. It had a forthright CEO and a junior partner who had been around since the company's earliest days, when their knowledge and contacts had been invaluable. Unfortunately, over time the CEO had progressed fast and the junior partner had lagged behind. Clearly there was frustration, and as the Roadmap was plotted and the plans developed, the CEO would often take me aside after our sessions and complain. Eventually (well, two or three months in) we decided that it would be necessary to buy the junior partner out. This entailed a new, hidden, parallel Roadmap, followed by various finance meetings and discussions about who would do what once the former partner was gone. When the arrangements were made and deals done, the SMT had to start the Roadmap again from scratch to accommodate a reshaped business.

It was a sharp reminder that the most senior team is not always the most cohesive, and that politics in the senior team can be much more damaging than anything below, because the latter can be solved simply by moving or removing people with little effect on the way the company is run. Entrenched politics or factionalism at the top require drastic surgery. The contest is never fair, and is rarely for the benefit of the business itself.

My second experience involved a head of department whose division was losing money. Their team was losing faith and had been for a year, and the person concerned had been over-promoted into their role. As a department head they were on the SMT. The SMT also constituted the Roadmap team. It was clear to me from the beginning that this person was out of their depth, with no hope of recovery. It soon became apparent to the other members of the group too. We found ourselves in the awful situation of skirting around the issue of cauterising the department when it was obvious that was the only solution to the issues at hand.

The conclusions were obvious. The team needs to be fresh-eyed, to come without preconceived solutions driven by back-room alliances. It should be made up of the best available: top performers, not biggest salaries. And ideally these should be the superstars of the future, representing the aspirations of the business rather than its ancestry.

A mix of more senior and more junior staff with differing skills but absolutely shared commitment is therefore ideal.

For this reason, in the companies we work with the group we put together is called the *growth lab team* (GLT) rather than the senior management team (SMT), which may also exist separately. If we were to simply include the whole of the existing SMT we would be exposing ourselves to big risks and roadblocks. These risks include:

- The expectation that at a certain level of promotion inclusion is a right
- The inclusion of senior managers who are effective at what they do day-to-day but would hold back the sometimes radical changes required by the Strategy Map (e.g. the excision of their own department!)
- The exclusion of up-and-coming superstars and thereby not having the input of the next and subsequent generations of management or leadership

While a team of up to nine can be effective, five (plus a chair) is optimal, because the Strategy Map usually results in around twenty tasks or projects to be delivered in the first year; twenty divided by four quarters and five growth lab members means one task per person per quarter.

This team will learn to expect complete delivery of each agreed task each month, will become adept at assisting one another in delivering projects outside their respective day-to-day roles or specialisms, and will eventually find they hold each other to account very effectively.

By building the 2Y3X Roadmap within the GLT rather than imposing it on them, and by formally reviewing stages of activity as a group of peers every month, you will create ownership and a high-performance team that can and will achieve the ambitious growth targets that have been set.

The 2Y3X Roadmap

The 2Y3X Roadmap is the tool used to store the information that comes out of the Strategy Map process. Specifically, it takes the tasks identified as being in the Strategy Map's Year 1 (highlighted in the diagram below), puts them in order of priority and dependency and spreads them out over Year 1.

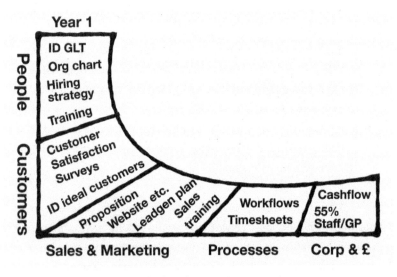

Tasks identified in the Strategy Map's Year 1

Q1		Q2	
Hiring strategy	Peter	Job scorecards	
Proposition	Kelly	Website, materials	
Timesheets	Samira	ID low-profit vs ideal clients	
Cust. satisfaction survey	Joe	Account Manager training	
Low-profit clients up or out		Etc.	
Etc.		Etc.	
Etc.		Etc.	
Etc.		Etc.	
Q3		**Q4**	

The 2Y3X Roadmap takes the Year 1 tasks, prioritises them and assigns them to the team.

The 2Y3X Roadmap itself is simply a single sheet divided into four, representing four quarters of the year, labelled Q1, Q2, Q3 and (predictably enough) Q4. Each quarter is broken into five spaces representing five quarterly tasks.

It is tempting to set seven or eight tasks in a quarter, especially if you have a number of people you would love to have on the GLT. Remember, however, that the output of a task is usually something that has then to be cascaded into the business as a 'This-is-how-we-now-do-things' change. People are generally extremely resistant to change, so it is much better to drip-feed changes slowly so that people get used to constant incremental improvement without feeling that the ground is shifting too rapidly under their feet. Instability breeds instability, and people will find other, more stable, places to work if they feel ill at ease. By only running five tasks concurrently, where it is likely that most are behind-the-scenes improvements or limited to single departments, the GLT will be making strategic changes without compromising culture or security.

Only one GLT member needs to be accountable for the delivery of each task. While sometimes a task falls naturally into an GLT member's skill set, often it may cross into several people's normal areas of responsibility. We are, however, only looking for one owner for each task, and 'accountable' does not always mean responsible – you may be familiar with an RACI Matrix: Responsible (does the work), Accountable (approves the work), Consulted (expert or advisor), Informed (kept up to date). While there can only be one person accountable to the GLT and Roadmap for a task, there may be several others who are going to be responsible for delivering the elements that make it up.

Above all, every individual task needs to be delivered in addition to each team member's normal daily activity. Nothing you are doing here in the growth lab excuses you or the team from doing your normal job, delivering the service or products to clients and managing your people. In order for this to be possible without requiring extra work that interferes with someone's personal life (which should be sacrosanct), each task must be small enough to fit into the spaces usually reserved for inefficiency! Task design must accordingly take this into account, or your superstar GLT members will feel overworked and under pressure. In practice it is far better to design each task so that it is small and easily doable over a longer time than to make it chunky and have a risk of it not being delivered or being done so badly it fails.

Finally, the quarters are split into months. In testing over several years, marking progress against the quarterly task as 'Red', 'Amber' or 'Green', or giving each task a percentage score, produces inconsistent results. The solution is to use a simple phased approach. Each quarter is therefore broken down monthly into Month 1: *Researched*; Month 2: *Prototyped;* and Month 3: *Delivered.* Each stage must be delivered on time.

Researched means all necessary reading, research and discussion into the approach has been completed, and the approach agreed with the rest of the GLT either in a weekly catch-up or ad hoc. If the monthly meeting is led by an external board advisor, chairperson or other external consultant (which I strongly advise), then their expectation will be that the GLT arrives at the meeting having finished the research and come to some conclusions.

Prototyped means the approach has been written up and implemented with a test group (staff, customers, recruits, etc.) or installed on a trial basis, the results assessed, and implementation agreed. It may be that following the test the project has to be extended, in which case the task must be recalibrated and potentially split so it displaces a lower-priority task currently sitting in the next quarter. Learnings, changes that should be made, and recalibration and reassignment to the next quarter are all welcome discussions for this monthly meeting.

Delivered means the new process has been refined, based on the prototyping stage, built, documented, hired or installed, and is ready for or already in use. More often than not, a delivered project requires subsequent staff training, bedding in, continuous monitoring or maintenance. So while a task may be considered delivered from the point of view of the 2Y3X Roadmap, to ensure it's not just ticked and forgotten there must be a subsidiary process to monitor the continuity of its output. This becomes an agenda item for your existing operations meeting, and remains the responsibility of the person accountable for delivering the task in the first place (unless delegated properly to the relevant department head).

For example, most Roadmaps I've worked with include the task of devising an interview process to ensure you only hire A-players (this task is, by the way, described in detail in Chapter 3). In month one there is a book to read, month two sees draft scripts and processes being tested, and month three sees all those who hire people trained in the new method. As part of this third month the head of HR, who will have been briefed and consulted by the task owner, will be asked to create a recruitment handbook for future use. This new process now becomes part of a department head's day job. The buck has been passed downwards, the process has become business as usual, and whoever manages the HR manager holds them to account as part of monitoring their ongoing effectiveness.

Returning to the task briefing, for each stage the expected output must be described so that the team member knows what they are expected to deliver at the end of any given month. This can be tweaked based on real-world experience, but over time this will become both easier and increasingly accurate.

In fact, running the 2Y3X Roadmap process for a trial quarter – Q-Zero, followed by Q1–4 – allows the GLT to get the hang of setting tasks that can be done readily in the time allowed. It also allows the GLT to get used to the commitment to the process required, and for you to make early changes to the team if necessary. This first iteration will inevitably be somewhat loose, and the tasks ill-defined, but it is a necessary step in the learning curve. It will highlight to the team that future tasks must be more specific, with a clearly defined deliverable and stages that can be identified in advance, with progress gauged against the expectations set at the start of the quarter.

Setting a Q-Zero and knowing it is a trial run means there will be fewer failures in delivering tasks when Q1 officially starts the process. This is important: you need to build confidence that the process can work given time, and this will come from the team itself identifying what needs to be tightened up as early as possible, and therefore establishing how tasks should be designed for success.

Interdependencies

The problem with having a bunch of important tasks to carry out is not only that they will have an implicit order within their respective segment (do timesheets > identify unprofitable clients > triage clients), but also that they often have cross-segment dependencies and impacts. Certain tasks will need to be put into logical sequences to provide the foundations for systemic change.

On top of that, tasks may need to be prioritised by urgency, perhaps because they've been flagged in the SWOT. Sorting out credit control to drive short-term cashflow is a good example.

In the absence of other tasks with higher priority, you could start with *Manage out C-players*, as in my experience this is usually the quickest win offered by the 2Y3X Roadmap process (for more on this see the chapter on People, p. 63). Assuming you share the 2Y3X Roadmap with the wider staff, you may wish to rename this task as 'Get the right people on the bus' – which is the formulation Jim Collins came up with for making sure that everyone who shouldn't be in your company is managed out, and that everyone left definitely wants to go on the next stage of your journey with you.

Some of this sequencing might take place within a given segment, i.e. 'People'. For example, three discrete tasks, *Build a recruitment pipeline*, *Design job scorecards* and *Create A-player hiring strategy*, must be spread across three quarterly tasks in the following order, as each depends on delivery of the previous work:

1. Create A-player hiring strategy.

2. Design job scorecards.

3. Build your recruitment pipeline.

However, there will also be some cross-section dependencies, in this case crossing into 'Processes'. Thus there will need to be a new HR process, possibly broken down into two or three quarterly tasks such as *Identify recruitment channels*, *Install HR management software* and *Develop scorecard-based personal development plans (PDPs)*.

Very occasionally one task will need to jump the logical queue. This may be because there is an immediate threat or opportunity. One might require action due to client dissatisfaction and morale, which might be partially solved by letting the C-players concerned go immediately.

It's usually obvious which order things should go in. The biggest challenges are clear, and must be broken down into quarterly tasks that are easily deliverable over and above the growth lab team's day-to-day commitments. This may mean breaking a single task into two or three quarterly blocks, delivered over six or nine months.

Ultimately, these interdependencies can mean that the set of tasks you first identify as being of the most urgency actually take a year to deliver completely and properly. You may feel that's too slow. But by the end of it you will have a solid foundation for the recruitment and management of superstar employees.

Unity and performance

The 2Y3X Roadmap, by design, encourages ownership by the team that creates it. So how does it do that?

The process of creating the 2Y3X Roadmap distributes the decisions that go into its creation among the whole strategic team. The pre-work by the owner is limited to the direction of the company in terms of the company's purpose (i.e. the products and services it provides to its customers), and its financial targets (e.g. three times gross profit in three years, at 20 per cent net profit). The GLT comes up with a unifying 'soft' target and then works out what the critical steps are to achieve all of the goals by working backwards from the three-year deadline.

By working through all the required activities and setting them in priority order, taking into account dependencies within the activity plan, the team owns the output and takes responsibility for delivering each activity.

This avoids any risk of 'not invented here' resistance to tasks by any strategic team member. Including all members in the development process means everyone will have the opportunity to discuss long-term goals and options, and then focus in on the specific activities and actions that will be required to deliver the chosen routes.

Once the group has decided on broad requirements, and annual stages to meet them, and then discussed specific modules of work to reach the first year's milestones, it is asked to break the work into quarterly tasks. Each member then takes on one task. This task is further broken down into monthly stages: research, prototyping and implementation. Of course, these three stages will need to be adapted to the nature of the task, and some of these will be covered with specific examples later.

A monthly meeting is then held by the team at which progress against each stage is reported and discussed if necessary. This way the team holds each of its members to account. The team member who misses more than one stage deadline in a row is either the wrong person to be on the team or the task has been badly defined or designed. An underperforming team member can be replaced or the task size or length recalibrated. To some degree this accountability serves to ensure performance, and if the failure is attributable to a flaw in the task's design then very soon the design of future tasks will be optimised to fit within the three-month Roadmap cycle. In both cases you will get a rapid improvement in the effectiveness of the team and the 2Y3X Roadmap's efficiency in delivering progress.

There are several implications of this method: members of the team will have to learn to delegate effectively to their reports; the size of each quarterly task must be manageable in the context of the member's day-to-day work commitments; there must be no shame in not being on this team (and no glory in being on it); and there must be a process for ensuring that tasks, once delivered, are inculcated into the way you do things.

Developing team coherence

The 2Y3X Roadmap process has many self-managing aspects, fortunately even when, as sometimes happens, the company's leader isn't the greatest manager of people.

Here are some of the unintended – yet incredibly useful – consequences of the process.

Members help define each of the projects and goals.

The team learns what makes for a successful task specification. A good task is one that can be done in addition to the project owner's day-to-day role and fits neatly into the quarter's month-by-month structure of Research, Prototype and Deliver. Well-set tasks will also fit around external factors like resource availability, feedback loops and implementation timing.

Both during research and towards completion of each project, thought is required as to how to cascade any resulting processes and its impact on behaviour and culture.

What this points to is that projects must have a life after delivery, and that a great staff incentive programme, for example, will not have any impact if it lives only in the staff handbook. It requires management training, building into one-to-ones, appraisals and reviews, personal development plans, financial planning including cashflow, evaluation of unintended consequences on corporate culture and so on.

This consideration must be applied to all tasks. In every task, an important part of the delivery phase will be identifying the correct person to be accountable for the newly designed process in the company going forward.

The growth lab team works collaboratively without hierarchy.

The company's leader works alongside everyone else to deliver strategically important projects. This is distinct from line management, which is about getting the best from people as well as cascading change throughout the company.

The team holds each member to account.

Peer pressure rather than downward authoritarian pressure ensures an extraordinary degree of delivery. While recalibration and course corrections are normal for the group (in turn showing people that this is a normal function of good decision-making), failure to deliver is never acceptable. What becomes normal is replacing non-deliverers without question or emotion, thus maintaining a team that continuously delivers and therefore effects change steadily year after year.

This also leads to a collaborative, collegiate culture fostered at the top of the company, as culture starts at the top and filters down. Especially as the leaders of the future are likely to be in the growth lab team, this will end up permeating the company fairly quickly.

The structure of the meeting fosters a culture of listening.

Active listening breeds an understanding of bottlenecks, to task refinement based on staged learning. It facilitates reprioritisation, changes in focus that may require additional assistance by different members of the group and evolving tasks. It encourages an understanding of how considerations change as task delivery progresses.

Members of the growth lab team begin to understand the pressures and requirements of their peers' roles, something often missing in any company of more than about twenty staff, where one's focus tends towards one's own department's complexities.

Growth lab teams become extremely tight-knit groups of highly effective leaders and, more than that, genuine friendships are formed. The team realises, usually after the first year, that it has taken the delivery of almost all the strategically important projects for the company on its shoulders, relieving the company owners of the burden.

The distributed workload builds ownership.

While the owners still have to deliver their respective Roadmap tasks, the distribution of important initiatives releases them to focus *on* the business instead of *in* the business. In other words, they are liberated from being in the weeds so they can focus on the truly strategic work of the ultimate leader – market strategy, communicating the vision, corporate finance and M&A. 'It's amazing,' said one of the leaders I worked with at one of the most successful marketing companies in the UK: 'after about a year I suddenly realised I wasn't running the company any more – the team we'd built was.'

This all boils down to sharing the load. So while the 2Y3X Roadmap process is an exercise in taking the load off your back as a leader and encouraging your best players to take some of it on themselves, it could all get stuck right here. One of the things you'll have to teach the growth lab team, so they don't get bogged down themselves, is delegation.

Decision-making and delegation

Proactive change can only happen when decisions are made. And people tend to think of bosses or leaders as better decision-makers than themselves. They tend to pass the buck up the chain.

In reality, good decision-making is about having the self-confidence to be decisive. This comes from practice, and from having the freedom and permission to make mistakes. What great decision-makers know is that decisions are simply choices; that sometimes you get those choices wrong, and if you do you have to take responsibility and potentially make a second choice to correct the decision. It is critical, therefore, to monitor the results of a decision so that any course corrections (re-decisions) can be made quickly. The responsibility of the good decision-maker is to ensure you have sufficient information at all times, so you are able to make a choice you can be confident in, can communicate effectively, can action and can then evaluate.

The accuracy of decisions is based on your experience – either of making similar decisions over and over again, or of the changes likely to be required if you made the wrong decision. Everyone makes decisions differently. One person may require 70 per cent of the information to make an effective decision nine times out of ten; another may only require 40 per cent. Some have so little confidence they need 90 per cent – which leads to decision-making paralysis; the opposite leads to recklessness. It is something people need training for from the beginning of their career. And, of course, nobody gets that.

Training in taking responsibility for decision-making can be easily done through controlled delegation.

Firstly, keep in mind an observation about delegation: if everyone in a hierarchy is empowered to make decisions that can only affect their immediate surroundings, and those branching below them, then any damage caused by an incorrect decision will be limited in the effect it can have on the business as a whole.

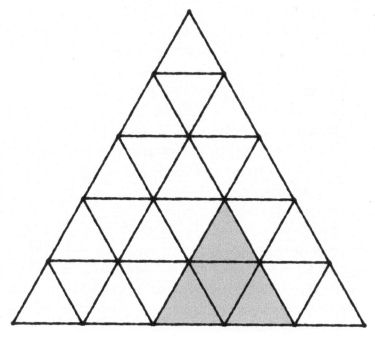

Learning how to delegate early means the effects of mistakes are localised.

If a decision could impact anyone outside one's own role and below, then it would be prudent to pass the decision up as many levels as is required to cover all areas potentially affected.

The opposite implication is that if you have a decision to make that will only impact the role and subordinates of one of your reports, then you should delegate the decision to them to make. In practice you will need to provide cover for your report, so they know you will be on hand for help (though not to make the decision itself) in case things go awry. It's the equivalent of a parent hovering behind a toddler as they learn to walk and run: it's fine to let go – for you as well as them! – and it's fine for them to fall, as long as you're there to help them up, reassure them, and help them keep trying until they gain the confidence to do it without your presence.

The simplest way to do this with the nervous novice is to delegate a decision while pointing out the limits of the damage that might occur if the trainee gets its wrong; then defining the precise parameters of the decision; then when to check in. The conversation might go something like this.

Manager: 'What can I do for you, Sandy?'

Sandy: 'We have a situation: X. What do you want me to do about it?'

Sandy is trying to pass the buck up the chain, to you. Your job is to pass it right back.

Manager: 'What are the options?'

This moves the discussion into neutral territory. (Classically a micromanager would at this point listen to the options, make a decision based on their own experience for the sake of speed and move on. However, this teaches Sandy nothing other than how to pass the buck.)

Sandy may actually not know what the options are. If so send her away to work out some options: 'Tell you what, Sandy, can you come back to me with three options in an hour?'

Sandy: 'A, B and C . . .'

There are two possibilities at this point. The presented options include one or more viable solutions, or Sandy has missed the only solution(s) that might work. You have a choice: let Sandy try one and fail; or send her away to come up with a few more. One way of phrasing such a request for further thought might be, 'OK, I think you might want to look at a couple of other options too. What would the boss do, faced with this decision? What factors might you have missed? Have another think and see me in an hour.'

Once you have decided whether to let Sandy try and fail before trying again and succeeding, or to encourage deeper thought, once again you put the ball back in her court.

Sandy: 'A, B and C ...'

Manager: 'What do you think we should do about it?'

Sandy: 'I don't really know. That's why I came to you!'

Manager: 'If you had to recommend one, which would you recommend?'

Sandy: 'I think B would work.'

Manager: 'How will you know if it's working?'

Sandy: '1, 2, 3 ...'

Manager: 'And what signs could you look for that would tell you if it wasn't going to work?'

Sandy: '4, 5 and 6.'

Manager: 'Great. Try it. Why don't you check in with me tomorrow morning at ten and let me know how it's going?'

Job done. That's all delegation takes, and delegation is all it takes to train great decision-makers. Your role is to facilitate their own information-gathering, develop their critical evaluation and build their self-confidence. Yes, we all know you can make the decision faster, better, cheaper, but if you continue to do so, you will be stuck making other people's decisions for them forever, and never be free to make the big decisions that only you can make, the ones that will impact the entire company and build your future success.

Anyway, all of the above boils down to what legendary hotel CEO Bill Marriott described as the seven most important words for a leader:

'I don't know – what do you think?'

The growth lab provides an ideal format for owners to start developing extraordinarily capable leaders of the future. Using this technique for your 2Y3X Roadmap tasks presents an ideal opportunity to practise the skills of delegating. The risks of this going wrong are mitigated in several ways:

- Tasks are already calibrated to be small enough to be delivered in a single quarter, and therefore the impact of getting one disastrously wrong is limited by its scale.
- The brief for a given task is originated and agreed by the GLT as a whole, so a clear understanding of the requirements is likely to be high.
- Tasks are broken down into three phases: research, prototype and implement. For a delegated task to be allowed to affect the entire business it has to go through two phases of testing and GLT approval before it is implemented for the entire company.

Another benefit of using the GLT as a testing ground for delegation is that not only are the risks minimised but the success rate is also likely to be high. This will give GLT members greater confidence in their ability to deliver, and lead to increased autonomy.

By extension, by learning how delegation works within the team, members will start to practise this with their own colleagues and teams, distributing both autonomy and decision-making skills throughout the entire company.

Bayesian inference

Where some risks are understood and decisions can be make-or-break, you need all the help you can get. Usually we ask our significant others. But sometimes a little maths can give you even more confidence.

Bayes' theorem is a modelling tool for statistics, and while it is complex enough to fry my brain a bit every time I've tried to get my head round it, a derivative tool, Bayesian inference, can be used to give a rough idea of outcomes based on a hypothesis plus some evidence, and facilitate decision-making. Here goes, then . . .

$$P(H|E) = (P(H) \times P(E|H)) / ((P(H) \times P(E|H)) + ((P(\sim H) \times P(E|\sim H))$$

It looks ghastly unless you're a maths guru, but it turns out to be pretty simple in theory:[10] the probability of an event happening is based on the likelihood (best guess) of it happening, and the likelihood of it happening given some additional evidence, tempered by the likelihood of the new evidence having a given effect.

Let's use an example to gauge whether a startup founded by an experienced entrepreneur is likely to succeed if it wins customers. On the face of it you might guess that:

1. Experienced entrepreneur doing startup = positive chance of success.

2. Wins customers = positive sign; therefore

3. Balance of probabilities says the startup is likely to succeed.

I spent much of my career coming to this kind of gut-feel decision, calling it logic. Bayesian inference gives you the tools to be significantly more precise:

- $P(H)$ = Likelihood of the startup succeeding given prior successful startups = 70 per cent
- $P(\sim H)$ = Likelihood of the startup NOT succeeding = 30 per cent

And given new evidence in the form of winning some customers:

- $P(E|H)$ = Likelihood of winning customers if the startup is going to be successful = 90 per cent

---

[10] https://en.wikipedia.org/wiki/Bayesian_inference for the full details, or read this great article by Pedro G. Del Carpio at
https://medium.com/@pedrodelcarpio/improving-our-beliefs-the-bayes-theorem-9d360a9a44fd

• P(E|~H) = Likelihood of winning customers if the startup is NOT going to be successful = 40 per cent

Therefore ...

P(H|E) = (70 per cent x 80 per cent) / ((70 per cent x 80 per cent) + (30 per cent x 20 per cent)) = 56 per cent / 62 per cent = 90.3 per cent

And the new company looks *really* good to go!

Of course, it does depend on a more or less accurate estimation of the probabilities concerned. However, as a ready reckoner for critical decisions it can be incredibly valuable, and the more hard data you can put into it the more accurate it will be. The reason I like this is that it can give you more confidence than your innate self-belief, and correct some of the misapprehensions about risk that plague leaders who often have fewer checks and balances than their less senior colleagues.

The big red button

One evening I was walking down Charing Cross Road in London towards Trafalgar Square. It was dark and the weather was a bit miserable. Most of the West End of London is pretty well lit, even up high towards the rooftops, and I happened to glance upwards.

Smoke was pouring out of a top-floor window, perhaps four storeys up. Pulling my phone from my pocket I ran into the pub on the ground floor of the building. 'Fire!' I shouted. 'Everybody out! There's a fire!' A few customers turned towards me, but otherwise all I got was blank looks. I headed to the bar and shouted again, and again got blank stares from automata staff. They thought I was nuts. Frustrated, I hunted around until I found one of those red fire alarms you smash with your elbow, and did just that. I tried to clear people out, but it took the alarms blaring before a single person reacted at all, and even then they thought it was a huge nuisance. I also called the fire brigade.

Two minutes later the siren came, and seconds later a huge red fire engine was parked diagonally across the pavement, uniforms pouring out of it. A huge man (I'm six feet tall; this guy was enormous) came over to me in his yellow trousers and braces as the orderly chaos unfolded around me. Was I the one who had called it in? he asked me. I nodded, as hoses were unfurled and instructions were being shouted. 'Here – when I say so, hit this button!' He pointed to a big red button on the truck. At his word I did so, and the fire engine's stabilising feet came out and planted themselves next to the wheels. From then on it was swift work for the ladders to be raised, pumps started, the building cleared, and the all-clear to be called.

No-one said another word to me. Certainly nobody who had been in the pub, working or drinking. Nobody asked me what had happened, and nobody acknowledged me.

Except.

Except the fireman. That one man who had given me a tiny role: *push the big red button*. It's entirely likely the button was a placebo. I was in my mid-forties; I should have been cynical. Whatever. But by explicitly associating having called the fire brigade with a reward that was at once both trivial and profoundly tied to every boy's dream of growing up to be a fireman, that man made it an utterly unforgettable life event. That tiny gesture was worth more than all the thanks, praise or reward I could ever have received from anyone else. I will remember that moment my entire life.

It taught me a huge lesson. Two, in fact.

The first and worst was that people are indifferent. Most simply do not care about anything other than their undisturbed pint. So when they do, you should recognise it.

And the second was that if a reward is designed properly it doesn't matter if it's big or small. If you design rewards around what is meaningful, they will be worth far more than monetary compensation. It's like acknowledgement: the right word from the right person at the right moment is usually worth more than gold.

Incentivising the growth team

The growth lab is, to some extent, its own reward. Superstars in any company will relish the chance to be involved in the strategic direction and future growth of their employer. It is dynamic, stimulating and important work, meaningfully measured, and confers non-line-management responsibility sometimes very early on in members' careers. It also looks fantastic on a resumé.

However, I am also a big fan of sharing the spoils of growth. You've got your company to where it is today, but you won't get it to where you want it to be – where the Strategy Map indicates you will be – without the help of a stellar team.

I do want to be explicit about separating incentivisation of managers from members of the growth lab. One of the mistakes leaders and owners frequently make is trying to tie management incentives to company performance. This never really works well: how do you decide who is worth a bigger bonus between the finance head who drives profit and the customer service head who maintains customer revenue, or the head of product who makes the high-quality stuff customers want to buy? Who contributes more? Or less? In my view managers should be incentivised based on the performance of their team (tracked and assessed through scorecards, covered in a later chapter) and on their own scorecards. Company financial performance is down to the strategic team, the growth lab Team. Their incentives should be unequivocally bound to the company's performance against its Roadmap and Strategy Map targets.

The growth lab team should be incentivised in the medium term, preparing it for long-term inheritance of the reins of the company as you approach your exit (whether it's moving on to a new firm, selling up, becoming director emeritus of a department you're passionate about, or setting up overseas).

Share options are a great way of providing an incentive. These can be set up so they accrue if certain criteria are met: Roadmap milestones, length of tenure, exceeding personal scorecards, corporate financial success, etc. You don't have to give away what you've already built – far from it. But you should consider giving away a meaningful chunk of equity in the additional value they will build from here on out. In other words, say you've built a company worth three million, and the goal of the Strategy map is to increase that value by a further four million: you decide to give away half of the incremental value to the team at the moment the Strategy Map goal is reached. They get two million to share (£400,000 each), you get your original three, plus an additional two. The share of the success is spread around appropriately, and the incentive is sufficient reward to make the effort not only exciting to be a part of but also financially rewarding.

This kind of approach to rewarding the growth lab team is more about proper acknowledgement of the team members' role in the holistic growth of the company than their role in managing their reports or departments well. Share options aren't money. They only mean anything in practical terms if and when the company is sold for a greater valuation than today's. But share options are a great signal of your appreciation; a red button, if you will.

Variations on this include proportionality based on length of tenure within the growth lab team if personnel changes, and perhaps cash bonuses but not shares – wherever possible you want to keep a shareholding list simple to make a future sale uncomplicated for the acquirer – for good leavers who have consistently hit their targets.

Ultimately, if the idea is to exit through selling your company, having a well-practised management team in the form of the growth lab is of huge benefit to the acquirer. While at exit it is likely that any share options will have crystallised, it will be easy for an acquirer to continue to incentivise the team through and beyond the acquisition. Incentives may well last through and beyond an earn-out, so having an established precedent will lead to an easier incentivisation transition for all concerned.

In some countries there are specific tax breaks and vesting rules for share options. Dig into the subject wherever your company is headquartered. It will be worth it.

KEY TAKEAWAYS

- The growth lab team should be drawn from your company's superstars, not just your senior management team, in order to drive extraordinary results while building your potential succession team.
- The Strategy Map starts at the end – with the goals – and works its way backwards towards the current year, in five streams: People, Customers, Sales & Marketing, Processes and Corporate & Financial.
- The current year's tasks are put in order and become the 2Y3X Roadmap.
- Each task lasts one quarter and is broken down into:
  - Month 1, Research
  - Month 2, Prototype
  - Month 3, Implement
- Improvements in decision-making come from being allowed to fail.
- Delegation risks are self-mitigating if you limit the consequences of failure to those downstream of the assignee. In other words, a junior's bad decision will have small consequences. So start practising delegation early, and you will grow a team that takes responsibility seriously and makes decisions well.

3

People

The people priority

It took me years, if not decades, to get my head around managing people properly.

I was one of those people who could see into the future sufficiently well to identify interesting opportunities and occasionally take advantage of them. I mean, we're entrepreneurs – that's what we do, right? And I had sufficient abilities as a communicator to inspire people to follow me into the unknown, and as a salesperson to be able to generate millions in custom from really big clients. I was the visionary leader type. And in the beginning I was utterly rubbish as a manager.

I remember the first time I broke a valued staff member. I treated someone as an object instead of a trusted (but no longer needed) colleague. I remember all those awful times when I treated someone badly because I had never been well-managed myself, and nobody had taught me. Worse, I had never realised that in the absence of all of these things I should have made the effort to learn how to do it adequately. My early journey as an entrepreneur was littered with mishandled management situations, all of which could have been dealt with better had I only taken the time to read a book or two.

I'd still never claim to be a natural manager, even after a successful twenty-five-year career. However, I've been fortunate in discovering that there are several tools which make it infinitely easier to help people to blossom in their careers, while at the same time becoming more useful to your company. Chief among these tools are the simple one-to-one agenda: ten minutes of getting to know you, ten minutes of your agency, ten minutes of my agenda – once a week.

To get where you've got to today, your vision, charisma and demands of your staff have been critical. To get where you want to get to in the next few years you will need much more, including the alignment of your employees and colleagues. It is so much easier to attract and hire those who already want to go on a journey with you towards a common future than to try and force them to change direction and do it your way.

Above all, though, you need brilliant people. I've had brilliant people who were trying to go off in a different direction. I've had brilliant people who didn't share my values, and as a result our personalities clashed. I've had brilliant people who disagreed with my vision and leadership so violently that they became a 'Pied Piper', turning entire departments against the company's leadership. The only way, by the way, to cure that disease is to fire the entire department. That kind of toxicity, if you've allowed it to manifest itself at all, can't be cured, only cauterised. Sometimes, brilliance on its own isn't all it's cracked up to be.

Brilliant people means brilliant people who will fit. I've shown the Strategy Map to potential hires and found that occasionally someone will tell me they don't see themselves at a company that's three times bigger. And I've also found superstars who want to be part of the journey, who want to help shape it, and who can visualise themselves standing with you when you get there. These are the ones you want.

Roadmap examples

In terms of the Strategy Map, the issue of high-quality staff comes up with almost everyone I work with. Here is an example of how it might be articulated in the People section of the map, where items in bold in the Year 1 column become actions for the quarterly roadmap:

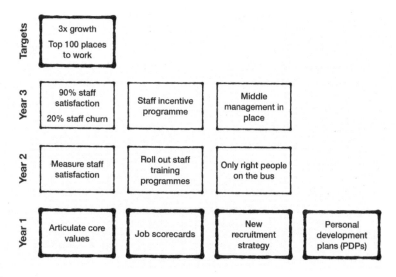

Roadmap example: people

There is a strong connection between staff quality and company growth. In simplistic terms, better-motivated staff are likely to make fewer mistakes that lead to revenue loss. As a consequence, assuming you also address sales and improve the new business pipeline, the company's revenue will increase.

The fuzzier – but probably more impactful – truth is that better people are happier people, and customers like working with happy people. There is consequently a link between the People segment and the Sales and Marketing segment of your 2Y3X Roadmap.

In the previous example of setting a unifying target of being recognised as one of the *Sunday Times* 100 Best Companies to Work For, you can further reinforce employee engagement and motivation through a series of nested activities and focus areas:

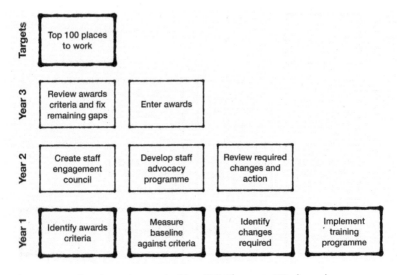

Roadmap example: Top 100 Places to Work goal

Each of the actions required in Year 1 then can be turned into a task with a measurable output, and an outcome that leads you towards your goal of being an exceptional place to work. You will of course have to prioritise them, and be mindful of the dependencies between the different segments, and also of the workload; you may find that something you'd like to get done in Year 1 must more realistically be sorted in Year 2.

The following example shows a more general approach.

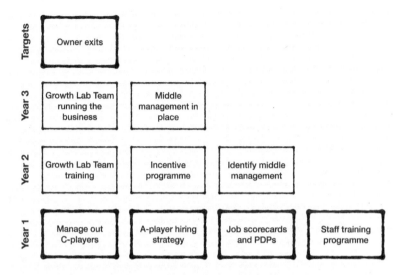

Roadmap example: Preparing for exit

Identifying core values

When starting the Strategy Map with your new growth lab team, it is a good idea to revisit the foundations on which you will build the company's growth. This doesn't mean previous work has to be thrown out: on the contrary, brilliant positioning, if it exists, should be retained and reinforced. However, long experience shows that, at the very least, your core values should be revisited.

'Core values' is not just a set of words to be added to the website to show customers, peers, partners or prospective employees what we would like them to think of us. Far, far too often you will come across corporate websites that espouse worthy but anodyne values, chief of which (usually) come phrases like 'The customer comes first,' 'Striving for continuous improvement' (copied straight from Amazon), or 'We treat our employees with respect.'

In essence these are bland and meaningless, reflecting what people think they should say, rather than what they truly believe and what truly motivates them as human beings.

The simple rationale for revisiting this properly is that you have a new team in place. As with growing a crystal, the shape and quality of the originating crystal will set the template for all that follows: woolly, out-of-date or imprecise definitions of what constitutes 'the way we think about things around here' will lead to ambiguity in values-based decision-making both within the growth lab team and outside it. In turn this will lead to an anything-goes culture: what is tolerated becomes acceptable; what is acceptable eventually becomes the way you do things. If the leaders believe that 'We should always strive to be better,' but you fail to communicate specific targets clearly and often or reflect it in your culture, then they will be just empty words, and not a hallmark of your organisation.

So, as the first exercise for the new team, you need to identify your core values.

A short one- or two-hour exercise will easily establish the true core values of the growth lab team. Ideally this requires an external facilitator: either someone you work with as an impartial non-executive director, or a specialist who can do this as part of delivering a newly articulated corporate proposition. The reason for an external facilitator is simple: they will use coaching techniques to draw out the real meaning behind the words people say. For example, one of the most frequently used value words I hear is 'integrity'. This can mean many things. My job is to unpack it and work out what the speaker really means by it. It could mean:

- Always tell the truth.
- Be honest.
- Be consistent with your promise.
- Uphold the highest standards.
- Behave ethically.
- Behave morally.
- Own your behaviour/situations/actions.

Clearly some of these need unpacking as well – what, for example, is meant by 'behave morally'? Whose morals? Religious, societal, personal? Who gets to decide? 'Always tell the truth': really? At what cost to the business? And so on.

In practical terms every person in the room should be asked to add their core, personal values to a list on a whiteboard or flipchart. As each word or phrase is added it should be interrogated for its precise meaning, unpacked and drilled down into until a precise term is identified that accurately reflects the intended meaning. This is done for each person in the room. Often you will find that some of the clarifications spark discussion. This probing is incredibly valuable, because it allows the participants to really get a feel for what each other member of the team really means. Each word or phrase is highly personal, sometimes reflecting deeply held personal beliefs and principles.

The following is a set of words from a team I met for the first time less than half an hour before doing the exercise. The illustration shows the progression of the word 'cloud' in two dimensions: as I went around

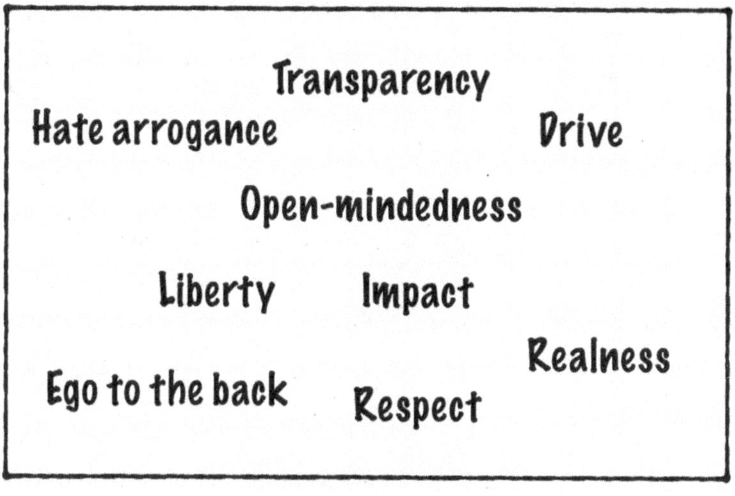

Identifying core values 1

the room for the first time getting each person's initial suggestion; then as they took inspiration from each other and expanded on their thinking.

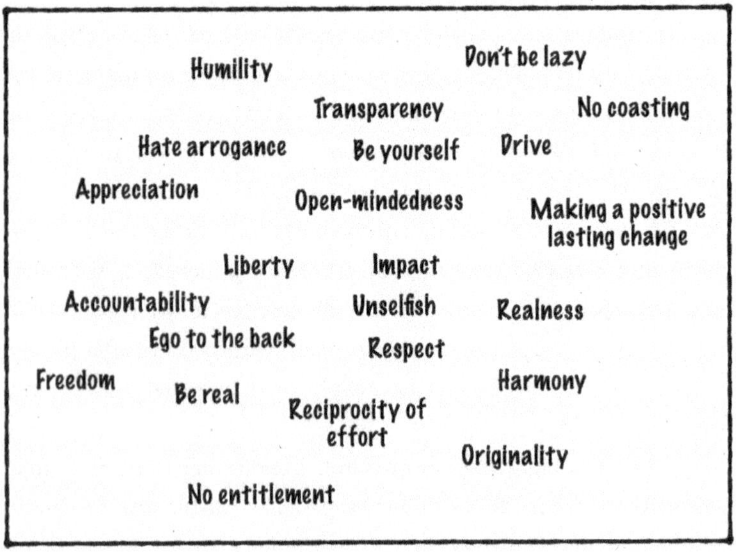

Humility   Don't be lazy

Transparency   No coasting

Hate arrogance   Be yourself   Drive

Appreciation   Open-mindedness   Making a positive lasting change

Liberty   Impact

Accountability   Unselfish   Realness

Ego to the back   Respect

Freedom   Be real   Harmony

Reciprocity of effort   Originality

No entitlement

Identifying core values 2

This is quite an exposing exercise, requiring skilled facilitation by an experienced and sensitive coach, and in practice this will be a bonding exercise.

The second part of the core values session is about finding common ground. I've found that the easiest way to reduce the number of words and phrases down to just those core values that are common to the entire team is by a show of hands. Picking one word or phrase from the board at a time, and with a preamble that there is no judgment in what follows, everyone is asked to raise their hand if they believe the idea resonates as a value they hold too – even if it's somewhat lower down on their own list. Very quickly you will find you reduce the field to a list of ten or so words and phrases, often fewer. Here you need to do a little more work to identify phrases that are similar in meaning or consequence. By consensus you will identify the phrase that is most powerful for the team as a whole. This repeats until you are left with three or four core values. These are then the consensus output of the growth lab team.

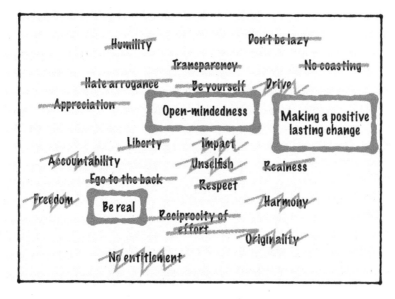

Identifying core values 3

What I have found repeatedly is that the team members look at the new list and realise it truly resonates with what they believe. But it also reflects several other important attributes of the way you want the business to work in the future. Here are some commonly recognisable reflections of these new core values:

- Our C-players don't believe in these values.
- Our A-players do.
- We wouldn't want to work with clients who didn't want us to behave this way.

- We wouldn't want to work with partners who weren't congruent with these values.
- We shouldn't be hiring people who wouldn't believe in these themselves.

The reason we do this exercise to identify the core values of the people in the growth lab team is so we can identify what is true of them. And identifying this truth allows us to be consistent in how we behave – both as a team and as a business. What you expect in terms of behaviour must be consistent for everyone in your business. Exceptions (for those who secure brilliant sales results, for example) just seed inconsistency and undermine trust. If you believe, as I do, that coherence – integrity – leads to trust in our colleagues and that in turn leads to confidence, then the business will thrive, because confidence is attractive to customers, A-players, partners and potential acquirers alike.

Once you have a baseline of truth you can consider your business's proposition in the context of your (true) values. Proposition is an important topic that will be dealt with later in this book.

As a quarterly task: core values

This is one of two exceptions to the usual quarterly task, inasmuch as it is usually done before the 2Y3X Roadmap gets going. Followed by proposition development, it is ideally done in a workshop format, and often includes workshop members outside the growth lab team, including, for example, your head of marketing, head of sales, and perhaps the company's senior management team. The reason we do this with a broad team is so we can be certain that the resulting values and proposition will 'land' – in other words, because they are truly foundation elements of all sorts of things to come, including marketing strategy and hiring policies. It is important that there are no high-level critics of the conclusions. Much easier to include key stakeholders, so that even if they are not included in the GLT they have at least been party to the groundwork the GLT will be operating from.

If the work is done prior to the Roadmap commencing, then it makes for a faster start for the remaining quarterly tasks, many of which depend on articulating the values and proposition. However, there is a quarterly task that can be implemented:

Task
Month 1 – Research

- Understand the role of core values in managing people going forwards.
- Decide how to communicate the new core values internally. For example, should you delegate the task of working out what each of the core values could mean to each individual in the company? Or should this be done through team-level discussions? How might you hold people to account?
- How and where should the core values be published internally?

Month 2 – Prototype

- Based on the outcome of the research phase, perhaps create a working group to start communicating the core values internally.
- Gather feedback to validate the effectiveness of the approach (or not).
- Establish a plan for wider roll-out.

Month 3 – Implement

- Roll out.
- Delegate responsibility for ensuring there is constant communication of and about the core values.

- Integrate the core values into the staff handbook and job scorecards.

Gathering your team

People are your foundation. Great people will help you soar. Mediocre people will bog you down. Bad people will drown you.

You have already identified your superstars, and you have brought some of them onto your growth lab team. That's a great start. In my view, once you know what your company is going to do, getting the 'who' bit right is the single most important thing you can do. On the Strategy Map it is therefore the first section.

'We can't seem to get anywhere. Every time I think we have customers happy, something goes wrong . . . Either we screw up in delivery, or a good person gets a better job somewhere else, or I have to spend my time geeing folks up. My people just aren't good enough to get on with doing it right without me breathing down their necks!'

I frequently run into this kind of situation – lacklustre people who seem to have been in place forever. And it's not just the problem of having mediocre people in the company: the main issue is that they tend to hire people who don't make them look inadequate. The old adage that 'B-players hire C-players' is true. B-players fear they will be shown up or bypassed by the juniors they bring into the company, and fear is a huge motivating factor for humans. So their natural tendency is to recruit people at or below their skill level, and that inevitably leads to degradation of quality over time, stagnation and a lack of capability to grow. I'm sure this is familiar.

The job of the great manager is to hire great people. In fact, the first rule in *Harvard Business Review*'s guide for managers is, 'Hire people who are better than you and let them get on with it.'

While B-players hire C-players, A-players hire other A-players. They are not afraid to raise the standards in the company. In fact, hiring great people is seen as a positive reflection on them. And provided the manager is good at delegation, bringing on better staff actually liberates them to progress their careers.

'Hey, boss – have you got five minutes?' – and boom, a pivotal staff member would be off to a competitor. It always filled me with a sense of dread, and in twenty years of building and running my own startups, it's this one sentence I can point to as the being the harbinger of stress.

After a few years, however, having hired some seriously great people and gone on a few coaching courses, I came to a revolutionary conclusion: everybody leaves.

This changed my whole perspective. If I knew that everyone was going to leave after, say, three or four years, then I should plan for it, and make it the best three or four years of their career. This idea has a fundamental impact on the culture of a business. Suddenly, rather than tempering staff progression, we started encouraging it. Instead of giving out a promotion every year or eighteen months, we would train people constantly, provide coaching, and accelerate their development. This obviously requires great people coming in at the bottom, so hiring A-players became mandatory.

The benefits should be obvious, although all my common sense seems to have come from making mistakes or from the blindingly obvious being pointed out by someone else:

- Great people in a great environment spread the word to others like them, and they don't tell average people about it because they only want to work with other great people. This has the added benefit of reducing recruitment costs.
- Rapid acceleration through training and coaching maximises engagement and focus on quality. Anyone left behind eventually disengages and washes out. The improving effect is somewhat Darwinian.
- Great training attracts those who are highly motivated in

their careers – new recruits are self-selecting as keen and driven. To be known as the employer of choice for the best in the business is attractive, not only to recruits but also to customers.

• Customers are exposed to high-calibre staff, which encourages repeat business (in other words, drives growth) as well as referrals.

• Morale is high so leadership stress is reduced.

Everyone leaves. But while you have them you have a highly motivated, highly trained, constantly improving team, attracting other A-players, reducing delivery problems, reducing customer churn, and enhancing your reputation in the market. This, for me, is the single most important change you can make in your business.

It does of course require discipline in hiring. I used to have a tendency to want to hire anyone with charisma or who did a brilliant interview. After a while the problems with this gut-feel approach became apparent: some turn out to be great; some terrible. It's not a very predictable art, hiring.

Rather than an art, it should be a craft. There needs to be a rigorous process.

How to hire A-players

According to Geoff Smart and Randy Street's excellent book *Who: The A Method for Hiring*, an A-player is: 'a candidate who has at least a 90 per cent chance of achieving a set of outcomes that only the top 10 per cent of possible candidates could achieve.'

All the best writing on this subject has been done by Smart and Street, so I would encourage you to read the book and implement it as far as you possibly can. But this also falls into the context of another great piece of advice from *Good to Great*: make certain you get the right people on the bus. You've decided that what got you here won't get you where you want to go next. Change is required. While you will re-centre on your growth lab team, inevitably this will mean you will realise some people no longer 'fit' the newly articulated core values.

The funny thing is, in my experience, these core values have always been there – they come from you, as a leader, after all. The recognition is more likely that some people never really did fit, and they are probably the ones holding you back the most. They may already be disruptive, provide bad examples or, worse, bad management, or even form the rump of your C-players. Although you may think it unlikely, I have often found that one company's C-player is another company's A-player – context, cultural fit and relevant personal motivation are critical to performance after all.

When you start to talk to your company about core values, these people will start to realise they are no longer exactly fit for your new purpose, and they may leave of their own accord. However, it is utterly critical that you remove your C-players as quickly as possible (as in: now). In my work with new clients this is invariably the quickest win with the highest impact.

Usually everyone on the growth lab team knows exactly who the company's C-players are. Removing C-players immediately not only frees up budget for the help you'll need building your Strategy Map, but is also a powerful indicator to the rest of the business that you're serious about making positive changes and building a better company.

Everyone, and I mean everyone, from the receptionist to the floor manager, knows who the laggards, shirkers and troublemakers are. They have assumed it's acceptable to be lazy or less than truthful or sexist, because nothing has been done about it. If you excise the tolerated-but-not-talented, standards across the board will inevitably rise. I pretty much guarantee that the day you do the deed, more than one person will remark to your face that they don't know why you didn't do it months – if not years – ago. And, to tell the truth, you're probably now wondering that yourself.

Once you've taken out the people who are holding you (and probably themselves) back, your focus must be on building a plan for filling your business with A-players. To summarise Smart and Street's conclusions, dismiss your reliance on gut feel and interviewer intuition in favour of the following four selection pillars:

- **The job scorecard** – describes the competencies required to accomplish a given role and the outcomes expected of it. This gives you a set of criteria against which you can evaluate candidates, then hold them to account once hired.
- **Source** – ensure that suitable or likely candidates are being pre-identified through your networks so you always have a high-quality recruitment pipeline when the need arises.
- **Select** – structure interviews so you can evaluate candidates against the job scorecard of the role you're hiring for and avoid what Smart and Street call 'voodoo interviewing' (by which they mean selecting candidates solely based on gut feel, personality or culture fit).
- **Sell** – means selling the job and your company to the candidate so they want to work for you above all others. Because it shows clear intent and ambition, I have found that having a structured Roadmap to show during an interview can be the clincher for real A-player candidates.

Job scorecards

A job scorecard is a powerful tool for identifying people who can do the work you want them to do and holding them to account while they are doing it. It is a simple set of metrics required for a given role to be successful. It might include financial, accuracy, quality or collaboration measures, for example. Each role will have a scorecard, and well-designed scorecards nest (so that a junior person meeting all their required scores will enable their manager to meet one of their targets).

Most people like to know what's expected of them, how they will be measured and what success looks like. Who knew? Scorecards give managers an early-warning system so they can make minor course corrections to their staff before too much time has passed and situations get out of control. By implication, with job scorecards by which employees are judged, continuous development via structured training aligned to the company's needs is vital. By introducing scorecards and training at the recruitment stage, you and the candidate can gauge whether they want to be on your journey with you.

Scorecards are always specific to both role and seniority. Here is an example set of required outcomes:

- Grow customer revenue by 50 per cent.
- Increase project margin by 15 per cent.
- Deliver monthly forecasts that are 90 per cent accurate.
- Close four £500K deals by the end of the year.
- Increase customer satisfaction score for 'on-time delivery' to 95 per cent.

At different seniority levels scorecards may be nested:

- Client director: deliver 50 per cent revenue increase from existing clients in twelve months.
- Account director: 90 per cent average aggregate customer satisfaction score.
- Account manager: every account delivers 20 per cent net profit.
- Account executive: 100 per cent customer satisfaction survey completion every month.

A scorecard for each role, while time-consuming to originate, gives a multi-dimensional tool for recruiting candidates who meet the A-player requirement (and for evaluating their ongoing performance):

- Is there evidence of the candidate achieving the scorecard in their previous roles?
- How does the candidate intend meeting the scorecard objectives in their new role?
- Is the candidate on track, or do they need assistance, training or course correction?
- Is the candidate successful in their role? (You might link annual bonuses partly to scorecard performance.)

The scorecard acts as a continuing benchmark of the expected performance of the employee. Use it in reviews, development plans and, if necessary, remedial work. Staying ahead of the curve is obviously much better than being behind it. I used to have a thirty-minute, one-to-one coaching session with every single employee once a month, which was extremely successful. Coaching isn't about teaching; it's about getting the person who is being coached to excel on their own account. You're just there to give them the space and structured encouragement to come up with their own ways of doing better. When done well, the progress is generated by the individual who is receiving the coaching. Coaching is entirely distinct from management in that regard. Actually managing someone requires monitoring, aligning, evaluating and improving sometimes through training, mentoring and direction. As a leader you can coach everyone. As a manager, well, bandwidth is the enemy until you've built a stellar team.

As I say, do read *Who: The A Method for Hiring*. In terms of Roadmap tasks that help you get the right people on the bus, you will need to get the task owner to read it too. I've found that a good exercise for the research month of a task is to read the book, summarise its key points, and have the summary reviewed by senior managers outside the team within the business. This will give you insights and inspiration for a solution that suits your business.

Isabel Odlin, a Growth Lab Team member at events and TV production agency Hub, produced one of the best scorecards I've come across. Her commentary is worth repeating here:

> 'We wanted to advance original scorecard thinking and find an approach to make outcomes more meaningful for individuals. With Deci and Ryan's self-determination theory in mind (autonomy, skills mastery and connection are needed to achieve psychological growth) we focused on allowing employees to own their growth and record their progress in a "growth map."
>
> Working with coach Charlie Warshawski we incorporated, managed, self-directed goal setting as well as self-awarded scoring. We gave our team leaders coaching to help them challenge and support their reviewees' progress against goals derived from pre-defined scorecard outcomes and role competencies.
>
> We segmented these goals into different areas around their core role, further learning, working practices and internal behaviours valued by Hub, and a "moon shot" (an additional, developmental contribution that will have a positive impact on the organisation).'

This is a great illustration of an underlying principle of 2Y3X and the Growth Lab Team: the job in facilitating the team is not to provide the answers, but to encourage critical thinking. In Hub's case Isabel came up with an entirely novel solution to the task, which perfectly suits the culture of the company and has therefore been adopted with enthusiasm.

Task

Month 1 – Research

- Read the book.
- Summarise key points and processes and circulate to stakeholders for review.
- Review current interview and job scorecard processes (if any).

Month 2 – Prototype

- Develop draft process for interviewing and use for current vacancies.
- Develop draft job scorecards for current vacancies and use for current vacancies.
- Revise current staff review process to include new scorecards.

Month 3 – Implement

- Develop scorecards for all current job roles. You might get department heads to help with this.
- Publish new interview process and train anyone who leads interviews.
- Integrate scorecards into staff reviews across the board.
- Hand ownership of the new standards and processes over to the right person – for example, your head of HR, or head of operations.

Three-year org chart

Having set the strategic goals in the Strategy Map, you know what kind of place your company will be to work, you'll know what quality standards you will be achieving, and you'll know your financial targets.

Set correctly and with sufficient ambition, your company will be significantly larger than it is today. If you were working with us at 2Y3X you would know you'll be at least three times the size. That's three times as many staff.

If you currently have thirty staff, you might at the end of this programme be approaching a hundred.

Despite my various attempts at implementing novel reporting frameworks, including zero-depth (flat) management and Holacracy or its variations, the reality is that it's difficult for one person to successfully manage more than about five reports.

If you have five direct reports, and each of those has five direct reports, the capacity of the company is twenty-six without adding a third layer of management. Having a co-founder at your side doubles the capacity, of course, but in order to hit your hundred you'll have to double up again.

The implication is that at some point you will need to institute a new management layer, which means that the most junior staff are at least one layer removed from your direct line of sight. Hiring, training, evaluating and developing junior staff will be down to a layer of people you won't have direct control over. So your A-player hiring strategy will have to be robust!

This growth will result at some point in departmentalisation and hierarchy. Too often I've seen this happen by accretion, making the company's structure haphazard or 'the way everyone else does it'. Some of the potential risks of this approach include:

- Staff being over-promoted to the level of their own incompetence (this is known as the Peter Principle).[11]
- Staff who might excel at becoming a better-trained do-er being put into a management position to which they may not be

[11] This concept was first described by 'hierarchiologist' Dr Laurence Peter and expanded on in the 1969 satirical book *The Peter Principle* by L. Peter and Raymond Hull.

suited, because there's nowhere else for them to be promoted to. This can be solved by identifying people as either management candidates or 'individual contributors' (read Rand Fishkin's fascinating book *Lost & Founder* for his experience of this).

• Departments which start with unified roles that need to be separated later, leaving a wake of destruction. When you're small, it often makes sense for account managers to also be project managers for service delivery, but when the two eventually have to be separated this not only breaks every process and workflow you've developed, but also disrupts staff career progression and morale as well as client relationships and client service.

Much better is to plan it in advance.

Given we have a three-year plan for the business, a three-year org chart makes perfect sense. By developing one which matches your company's three-year state you can compare it to your current set-up, work out who might go where over the next three years (which is fuel for career progression discussions, hiring briefs and job scorecards), and devise a plan to make it all happen.

Task
Month 1 – Research

• Review and bring up to date your current org chart.
• Work out what your company will look like in three years' time from the point of view of staff numbers, management bottlenecks and layers, departmental set-up in the context of likely product/service development, and individual roles within each department, as well as 'glue' roles (operations, administration, finance).

Month 2 – Prototype

• Draft your three-year org chart.

• Add all your current A-player staff into it assuming strong career progression (either as managers with growing responsibilities or as individual contributors).

• Identify potential training needs alongside assumed career progression.

Month 3 – Implement

• Incorporate career progression into individuals' personal development plans, set goals and KPIs and adjust job scorecards if necessary, and assign to someone to own the process going forwards.

• Identify key milestones for recruiting currently missing assets (new department heads or senior people, etc.), and assign responsibility (and budget) to the relevant person.

• Incorporate the likely costs into the budget forecast for the three-year plan.

• Establish a review timetable.

Staff training

There's a management cliché (and there are so many) that goes like this: 'What if we train our staff and they leave?' says one.

Replies the other, 'But what if we don't train our staff and they stay?'

If you're serious about hiring brilliant people, then you should get serious about retaining them. And the best people want to develop and improve. One of the key issues which usually appears in year one or two of the Roadmap is staff training. Many of the companies I've worked with have made at least a rudimentary start. Sometimes they'll have a training budget set aside – a few hundred per employee, perhaps. Usually this is used at the employee's discretion. Often this discretionary learning budget is spent on attending conferences where they can meet up with peers, or on vocational learning, or on adding skills to their CV in anticipation of some future move. While sometimes it is an indicator of what someone would really rather be doing, more often than not this random selection of upgrades based on having to spend a budget is counter-productive or neutral.

A good manager will be much more involved in the decision-making for their staff. Ideally all training should support several things:

- The future plans of the department;
- The personal development of the individual; and
- The company's policy of continuous improvement.

And in turn should take into account:

- Perceived weaknesses or opportunities for up-skilling the individual;
- Departmental weaknesses or opportunities; and
- The individual's professional development in support in future roles, possibly as defined by the three-year org chart.

The plans made at department or manager level need to fit into the context of your company's goals, and should support the Strategy Map as it develops over the three-year period. As such, staff training is a prime candidate for a Roadmap task.

Task
Month 1 – Research

- Review all current training.
- Map potential training opportunities to Strategy Map priorities.

• Map training to the three-year org chart, taking into account key staff progression and skills required for future positions.

Month 2 – Prototype

• Develop and cost a training programme with a long-term training schedule, and test feasibility with department heads and those responsible for resource-planning.
• Identify suppliers for each key training strand.
• Build a budget and initial period of training based on current needs.
• Develop a draft training plan and establish KPIs.

Month 3 – Implement

• Roll out first training modules and measure against KPIs.
• Establish a timetable to review success and tweak as necessary.
• Set a deadline for incorporating the training plan into the staff handbook and budget cycles.
• Identify the person who will be responsible for training for the company in the future.

You may also wish to consider getting yourself trained in coaching. Perhaps your senior team too. In an ideal world, everyone in your company would receive coaching of some sort, probably integrated (whole person) coaching at a senior level and directive or skills coaching at more junior levels. I loved learning how to coach, and then coaching my team. Watching the person you're with arrive at a sudden realisation of what they want to do next is one of the most satisfying experiences a manager can have. You may decide to include building a coaching programme as a quarterly task once the more structural tasks have been implemented.

KEY TAKEAWAYS

- Take time to identify and articulate the personal values you share with your team. (This will require external facilitation.)
- A-players are those who have 'at least a 90 per cent chance of achieving a set of outcomes that only the top 10 per cent of possible candidates could achieve'.
- Surround yourself with A-players who share your team's values and your culture will thrive.
- Use scorecards to define the expectations for roles, to measure each staff member's success against, and to hold people to account.
- Train your staff continuously – it's better to have brilliant people coming to you for training then leaving after a while, than to have stagnant people staying with you forever.

4

Customers

Keeping customers happy

Early in my entrepreneurial career the joke used to be that if only our firm didn't have clients or staff then life would be perfect. I used to dread those horrible words: 'Boss, we've got a problem . . .' – the key client suddenly withdrawing the budget, deferring the hard-won project, firing us out of the blue or ghosting us.

My companies had a dozen or so big customers, each managed by account handlers in daily or weekly contact, delivering meaty projects. But it's no different if you have a thousand (or ten thousand) customers licensing software from you, or buying your goods via e-commerce or physical stores. Keeping customers happy, whether in multi-contact or face-to-face or arms-length or digital relationships, is important no matter what you do. It doesn't matter whether you measure their happiness by how much they spend; by whether they come back again; by asking for direct feedback; by asking them to rate your app or your service; by reading their reviews; or by watching churn rates. To grow you need to keep your customers happy and profitable.

It's a fine balancing act. Successfully managing customer satisfaction relies on a degree of foresight coupled with a pragmatic view of where to focus your resources in order to improve your customer's perception of problem areas. To do this effectively you need to look at three separate areas as part of the Roadmap:

- Foreseeing problems;
- Identifying usefully profitable customers; and
- Delivering profitable work.

Delivering profitable work will end up being a process task rather than a customer task, although it will be made considerably easier if you address your customers' perceptions of your service, and if you take some care in selecting clients that will be both profitable and easy to work with. Both of these are important tasks and will be covered in this chapter.

Roadmap examples

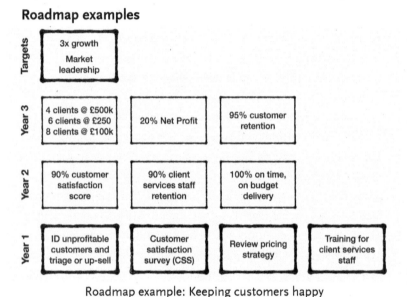

Roadmap example: Keeping customers happy

Some of the customer tasks involved in reaching your goal of happy customers will either require, or be driven by, tasks in other segments. For example:

- Customer satisfaction survey: highest-scoring customers should be asked for referrals (a sales and marketing task);
- Identify unprofitable customers: implement timesheet tracking and compare with what's charged to customers, and add this data to the monthly KPI report (process task); and

- 90 per cent client services staff retention: training for account management team (people task).

Heading off customer dissatisfaction

With demanding clients and limited resources, you need to be able to foresee problems and head them off so you do not end up constantly firefighting.

Early in my career I was once told something by a client during a review. It came after a period of increasing grumbling by the client about our attitude towards them, which my team felt was unfair. Eventually I was asked to meet the client and work out what was going wrong. The client and I sat down, and I asked for and got a whole bunch of feedback, most of it really positive. Confused, I finally cornered the client, and discovered that they felt that we weren't delivering sufficient value for money.

I was stunned. The team was delivering £19 of new sales for the client for every £1 they spent with my company. When I told the client this they too were stunned. 'I had no idea,' he said. 'We've been increasingly dissatisfied because all we could see was your costs going up!'

We'd forgotten that if you want someone else to understand something, you have to communicate it clearly rather than expecting them to guess. The client was dissatisfied because we weren't checking in on what mattered to them, making assumptions that they should be happy when, because we weren't clearly communicating, their perception was one of failure. 'Perception is reality' – it's a hugely important lesson in customer management that has stood the test of time.

Client satisfaction scores (CSS)

The easiest way to identify what a customer thinks is going on is to ask them. And yet people do this way too infrequently. Most of the time they are scared to; or they use methods that have a built-in bias, or which elicit responses only from the satisfied, or, most evil of all, which they game to boost their scores and fool themselves, their investors or their future customers.

In the UK, Steve Antoniewicz came up with a way to gauge customer satisfaction in the advertising world, by asking clients to rate their agencies anonymously. Each year every agency would ask its clients to rate its services using a simple survey of seven questions. Through Steve's platform (now part of The Drum Consulting) the agency could then see their aggregate scores, guess which scores came from which client, and hopefully work to improve its services. Those most highly rated by their clients would win awards.

From day to day you don't need to win awards. But you do need to know how to improve what you do. And you do need to know what your customers think of the services you provide. So you should be asking them. Often.

Here are the seven ratings The Drum Recommends is based on (scored as a percentage), bearing in mind its industry of marketing services and creative agencies:

- Client service
- Proactivity
- Strategic input
- Creativity
- Value for money
- On time
- On budget

Clearly this will need to be tailored to your own (industry and sector) needs. However, it is a really useful set of measures. I strongly recommend monthly surveys. Quarterly, end-of-project or annual reviews are simply not sufficient to gain an ongoing understanding of the ups and downs of your relationship, and neither are they sufficiently immune to 'getting the timing right' – gaming the results to make the surveyor look good. On which note, for some it might also be a good idea to have the survey done anonymously or by someone unrelated to the customer account.

By gauging a customer's current perception of the relationship with your firm, in a fairly clearly delineated set, we can easily spot patterns and trends. If a client consistently low-scores your value to them, then you will need to unpick whether that means you are failing to deliver value, the value is not of the kind that is required, or you're not communicating your value effectively enough. If several clients make the same observation, then again you know what to address – perhaps you need to refocus your service delivery, or only target clients who want value that's more in line with what your company can deliver. If a low score applies to clients with the same team in common, or similar types of brief, or who order on the same day each month or whatever, you will be able to see patterns and address them. No data, no improvement. Frequent data, and you can spot and head off problems before they become serious enough that the client calls in the supplier's CEO – you! – or, worse, simply drifts away.

Once you've done your first customer satisfaction survey you'll have a baseline. I would expect it to be quite high the first time out, but customers will find their level and start to score you with increasing honesty and directness once they realise it is to their benefit. Positioning such a survey is easy: 'If you tell us where there's room for improvement, we'll change things for the better.' You do, however, have to follow through and make improvements, and then report back to the customer in the context of their feedback so they can see it's not just a cosmetic exercise.

As the adage says, what gets measured gets done, and by focusing on customer or client satisfaction you will foster a culture that is open about reporting areas for attention and then taking action to improve.

	Low score	High score	Average
Client service	75	85	80
Creativity	50	85	67
Effectiveness	65	80	72
Professionalism	50	90	73
Strategic thinking	80	80	80
Value for money	65	75	70
Advocacy rating	80	95	85

An example using a standardised set of questions derived from
The Drum Recommends survey

Consistent low scores in any particular area highlight what you as leaders and managers need to do. Perception correction may mean additional reporting, presentation training, or a different feedback mechanism or even a team change. Actual fault correction may require staff training, for example, or finding better ways of working (process reengineering), or different suppliers. You may find new opportunities here too: a hole in your service may indicate a client need unaddressed, leading to new product or service lines, and even the acquisition of new talent or businesses.

From a customer perspective you will quickly acquire a reputation as a supplier who cares. The unexpected consequence is that you will often find you have more time to address and fix things that go wrong – a customer angered by a surprise or an unaddressed deterioration is much, much more destructive, I think, than a customer to whom you can report steady if slow correction.

It is so important a tool that the CSS score is one of the business KPIs reported in every 2Y3X Roadmap meeting. First the headline score, then any negative outliers or negative trends, so the team can interrogate what's been going wrong and the solutions can be reported or addressed if necessary.

Reporting framework

Customer Satisfaction Score overall	95%	Aggregate average across all measures
		Supporting pages/slides showing each customer's scorecard. This allows you to review any issues if necessary and provides an insight into your potential organic growth
% of customers responded	100%	Exceptions to be highlighted
Trends reports		13-month Line Chart of headline score
		13-month Line Chart of score by customer
		13-month Bar Chart of high-low score range by question. This will highlight problem areas as well as eventually giving you data on peaks and troughs during the year

Summary of how the CSS should be reported to the growth lab team each month

Task
Month 1 – Research

- Look at any previous customer satisfaction surveys you've done.
- Identify key areas that are of importance to your customers which could become scoring criteria.
- Ask key customers what issues they would like to see

monitored, and how they would like to be surveyed (bear in mind you need this data frequently, at least monthly, so it's likely the surveys will need to be quick and informal).

Month 2 – Prototype

- Draft a survey and test with key customers.
- Create a reporting format that will work for your business. Reporting should aggregate all scores and multiply the average result by the percentage of customers responding. This will give you an overall score, and mitigates the risk of the survey being gamed to only include high-scoring customers. For those with hundreds or thousands of customers, then the sample size needs to be statistically sound: 383 respondents will give you 95 per cent confidence in the score with a ± 5 per cent margin of error.

Month 3 – Implement

- Train the relevant teams in administering the survey and gathering the results.
- Roll out the survey to all customers or a representative sample.
- Collate the first response data and report to both the GLT and customer teams.

Identifying usefully profitable customers

Most customers require roughly the same amount of attention in order to keep them happy, no matter how much they spend.

In other words, whether it's a ten-grand client or a hundred-, a similar number of hand-holding hours will go into each. While project delivery may be perfectly scalable, customer service or account management is not. In an ideal Excel business plan each dollar of revenue has a fixed service cost attached to it. However, we all know that this is simply not borne out by practical experience. The bigger the customer, the more sophisticated they are likely to be, with higher-quality staff, and so the level of handholding, education and learning on the job is markedly reduced. While it may take ten people to look after a large client, it is very unlikely to only take one person to look after one a tenth the size. Profitability is not lineally scaled with the size of spend.

Each time we set out to win a new customer, it takes a similar amount of sales resource and marketing spend, no matter what the size of the win. This too adds to the unbalanced nature of scale versus profitability. And in a smaller company, that effect can be stark. Say it takes three people to look after a customer, and one person to win the customer. Twelve customers means one person for the time it takes to win each one, plus thirty-six people to maintain them once landed. Does it make more or less sense to spend more time winning a customer four times the size? One person to win them, but with four times the amount of time to do it in; nine people to maintain them once landed.

A different way to view it is this: assuming all customers net 20 per cent profit, would you rather have ten £500K customers or a hundred £50K customers? In a buyer's market or with only a few salespeople, which will be easier to scale?

On the flip side, in a service business with serious ambitions for growth there will usually be a truncated pyramid of sorts. Tier 1 customers will be big, long-term and likely to be accounting for around 50 per cent of the revenue base. Tier 2 are medium-sized with the potential to become big. Tier 3 are smaller, with the potential to move up the scale. Striking the balance with a focus on profitability, 'growability' – dependent on fit with your strategic plans, culture, future product evolution, etc. – and resource intensity is important.

Similarly, you need to be able to identify types of client that are sub-optimally profitable. For example, you might identify common factors in customers that are prone to changing deadlines or making last-minute changes to orders.

Triaging customers for profit

Clients and customers will have several attributes that affect their usefulness for you as a business. These could include:

- Cost to acquire
- Leadership team's effort to acquire
- Cost to retain
- Service level required to retain
- Resources required compared to resource scarcity
- Initial value
- Lifetime value (CLTV)
- Profitability

An important factor when I was running my own businesses was the likeability of the customer. On several occasions the list of customer names looked great, but the client was a pain to deal with; patronising, rude, entitled, or dumber than a drawer labelled 'Bits of useless string'. The morale effect of firing these otherwise superbly profitable customers always – and I mean always – outweighed the loss of revenue. And guess what? In retrospect all those awful clients shared none, not one, of our deeply held core values.

By creating a customer scorecard using data to hand or easily gathered, you will see a reflection of the 20/60/20 rule: 20 per cent highly profitable, low-effort; 60 per cent profitable, moderate-effort; and 20 per cent low-profit, high-effort. If you include all the considerations eventually you will find a 20/60/20 that takes into account all factors and produces a 'want more of', 'happy to have' and 'avoid more of' list.

In an ideal world you should address the 'avoid more of' list as soon as possible, in much the same way as you ought to address getting rid of C-players the second they have been identified.

One relatively easy and pragmatic way to do this is to play back to those customers the things that need fixing. It's simple, honest and polite and, if they fix those things, they may become great customers, promoted to the 'want more' category.

So if a customer is unprofitable, explain why, and suggest ways this could be fixed. Using timesheets in service businesses makes this relatively easy, but you could also work out resource costs to show where things are going wrong.

Don't forget that if a client makes you a small profit – say 5 per cent, and you'd rather make 10 per cent – then every percentage point you increase your price by goes straight to your profit. To get to 10 per cent you only need raise your prices by 5 per cent – which may not be much more than the prevailing rate of inflation. One way to look at the challenge this represents is to ask yourself whether by raising your prices by 5 per cent or even 20 per cent you would lose more than 5 per cent or 20 per cent of your customers. If not, then you may as well do it: it raises your average prices and increases your profit, while potentially reducing the number of unprofitable clients.

Regardless of the theory, in practice you should not keep clients that are unprofitable unless you have them for reasons of culture (i.e. charity or fun), stakeholder perception (corporate responsibility or industry regulation), or influence (high-profile customers who attract others that are profitable). The first and last are counted as 'fame-or-fortune' clients, and the *fame* clients are there simply to attract the *fortune* clients either now or in the future.

Of course, if a customer is just plain rude and can't be politely re-educated or replaced, then I'd recommend you let them go. Everyone concerned will be much happier, and your staff will love it that you've sided with them and not the money.

Picking customers for growth

In order to work out what kinds of customer you want more of, it's worth taking a long hard look at the 20/60/20 customer list. The top 20 per cent of your customers will share attributes with one another and with your own company, some of which are the foundation stones of a great business partnership or a happy and long-term customer relationship. In my experience, almost every company I have ever worked with in developing their proposition has noted that their best customers also behave in a way that is consistent with the core values of the growth lab team. But if you can identify one or more attributes shared by all the customers in your top twenty, then this gives you a very good idea of who you might wish to target going forwards. After all, if you can somehow find a way to have more dream customers and clients, why would you not put in the effort to do so?

As a quarterly task this one is usually quite revealing, and the required output is easily defined. The research phase will require data, which may necessitate a delay in starting the task. However, the results are usually remarkable, both for morale and resource efficiency. Your business will immediately be more profitable.

This work on identifying your sweet spot also gives your company some of the necessary ingredients for the section on sales and marketing, which comes next.

Task
Month 1 – Research

- Gather utilisation and recovery data (described in detail in the Financial and Corporate section p. 135–151) for each customer.
- Check profit total for each customer (even if it's a 20 per cent profit customer, 20 per cent of two grand isn't as useful as 20 per cent of twenty grand).
- Gather CSS data for each customer – both scores and response rates.
- Gather staff impressions and identify problematic customers as well as well-liked customers.

Month 2 – Prototype

• Create a customer list divided into keep, 'up or out' (make profitable/improve satisfaction/improve relationship or, if not possible, fire), and fire.

• Develop an 'up or out' plan for relevant customers.

• Identify elegant ways to get rid of unwanted customers. This might include finding a different supplier to hand them off to (a great way to make industry friends and potentially establish future partnerships), finishing the current work and closing it down, or upping your prices until the customer decides to find themselves another supplier.

Month 3 – Implement

• Implement 'up or out' plan.

• Communicate your decisions internally to ensure your staff know that you mean business about being profitable, successful and loyal to their satisfaction as much as your customers.

• Add common (positive and negative) indicators to your 'ideal customer profile' for use by your marketing and new business teams.

KEY TAKEAWAYS

- Understand what your customers value about what you do. Regular customer satisfaction surveys:
  - Tell you what your current customers value;
  - Tell you what you need to improve;
  - Give you insights into how you can improve the relationship, your products, your processes and your staff;
  - Give you the opportunity to develop new products and services based on what your customers actually want.
- Focus on customers who want what you do, share your values, and are profitable.
- Identify customer segments that will help you grow and focus on attracting more of them. These might be customers that have the potential for expansion, and therefore greater demand for what you do, or those that might want additional or related products or services.
- You will increase profit by stopping doing things that are not profitable. Get rid of customers who are not profitable, or change what you do for them so that it becomes profitable.

5

Sales and Marketing

Feast and famine

Too often I come across companies lurching unpredictably between too much work and too little. It's a problematic but unfortunately entirely predictable cycle:

'We have too much work on to be bothering with lead generation or pitches.'

'We don't have enough work – let's focus on lead generation!'

'What if we win all these pitches? We won't be able to cope, so let's pause for a while ...'

It can be catastrophic. Because you are constantly being reactive, based on your current resource availability, the waves and cycles sometimes coincide and overwhelm you. I have seen businesses win too much work, leave existing customers unserviced, lose those customers, and then go bust for want of sufficient revenue. In aviation terms this is called pilot-induced oscillation, and it can lead to a fatal crash.

The trick is to line up several functions and have them running in parallel at a pace that provides a predictable feed of new customers:

- Lead generation
- Qualifying in/out based on strategic, cultural and product fit
- Conversion (including pitching, proposals, estimating, closing)
- Onboarding
- Cross-selling/up-selling

Ideally these areas would be dealt with by specialists, but in practice in a small company of twenty or sixty staff this may all be handled by one or two people. In order to make things function well, you will need some reliable basic processes as well as a crystal-clear proposition so that you know what you are selling and to whom.

Roadmap examples

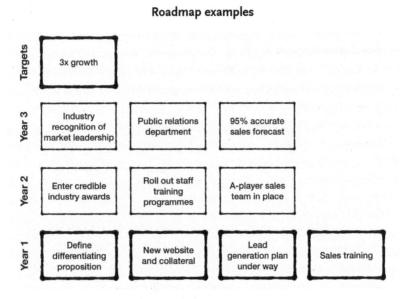

Roadmap: Sales and marketing

You can see that in this example the four Year 1 tasks have been put in a specific order. Hopefully it makes perfect sense why you'd do it this way – no proposition means nothing to take to market, no direction for leads, and no leads means no deals to close. Your own marketing strategy will be specific to your product or service and to your market. However, proposition development is so critical that it will be covered in some detail here. I know if you've built your company up this far you know how to sell, so I hope you will forgive me if I'm teaching grandma to suck eggs, but this chapter will also touch on how to sell value rather than price, and highlight some psychology-based selling tips.

Positioning your company in the market

Deciding on what makes your company different is the single most important thing you will do. What you come up with will be the guiding light of your firm. Jim Collins stated that the ideal positioning is at once something you can be the best at and something that can be defended. He called it the Hedgehog Concept, after the unassuming herbivore which when attacked rolls itself into a ball of spikes that can't be breached.

The Hedgehog Concept can be illustrated using a Venn diagram to describe the requisite attributes of a successful company:

Positioning your company in the market

The reason three-circle Venn diagrams are so powerful, by the way, is that they describe the minimum stable configuration. Two circles can be moved around willy-nilly, and the only stable relationship is the intersection. Three circles are stabilised by their relationships both with the intersection and with each other. Another way of thinking about this stability is to imagine it as a stool you want to sit on. Three legs, no uncertainty. In the above diagram, for stability you need all three to be true.

- *Passionate About It* plus *Good At It* is great, but without *Makes Money* you don't have a company.
- *Passionate About It* plus *Makes Money* without *Good At It* leads to customer dissatisfaction and no company.
- *Good At It* and *Makes Money* but not *Passionate About It* makes for dull and therefore uncompetitive and ultimately again no company.

To come up with great positioning – differentiated, defensible and a stable platform for marketing and rapid growth – requires not construction (which is artificial and will eventually be seen through) but discovery. It has to be genuine. You have to uncover it.

So where do you start?

Proposition

Having a crystal-clear proposition will tell potential customers if you're the right supplier for them and should set you apart from your competitors. Jaynie Smith, in her book *Creating Competitive Advantage*, describes what is required: *What's different about you, in the eyes of your customers, as distinct from your competitors*. 'A relevant competitive advantage', says Smith, 'gives buyers a reason to choose you over your competition'.

What you offer must resonate with the potential customer to the extent that when they decide they need something like your product or service, you are the supplier they should get it from. This requires confidence in your product or service, of course, as well as an adequately differentiating proposition.

The Hedgehog Concept states that what you do must be based on something you can excel at – ideally something you can be the best in the world at. In addition, this must be defensible. A great proposition lends itself to becoming defensible. For example the proposition, 'The creative agency for entrepreneurs' (which belongs to Alpha Century, a

London advertising agency), describes what the company does and for whom. It builds a requirement for a particular expertise into the way the company is run. The company makes it a practice to hire staff with their own entrepreneurial experience – for example creatives with experience running their own Etsy shops, or a head of project management with their own startup behind them. This increases their chances of entrepreneurial clients hiring them: there is a common language and a mutual appreciation of pressing business issues. This in turn allows them to further increase their expertise, putting them in an unassailable position as compared to their competitors. Alpha Century tripled its gross profit in two years, and went from a seven-person team pre-2Y3X to a top-forty advertising agency once we had defined the new proposition and they had completed the programme.

So that's the simple definition of what you should do as a business. It's about proposition, rather than simply product, and it must be:

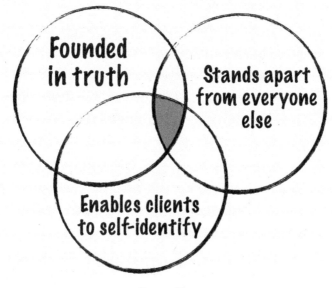

Founded in truth

Stands apart from everyone else

Enables clients to self-identify

Proposition

Founded in truth has two elements: the first is that you must be able to substantiate it, the second that it must be true to your team's core values. Substantiation really sits in the claim that you are or can be the best in your market at something. This element of the proposition has a secondary benefit: if you make a strong claim to be the best at something, then you must align your work processes and one or more strategically important projects with sustaining your competitive advantage. In other words, if you are to focus on creating fame for a proposition that marks you as the best at something, then your business must be oriented around continuing pre-eminence in your field. This might require continuous innovation, paying a premium for the best talent, and a focus on peer, client and industry recognition. It would therefore be prudent to examine the implications of a particular claim or aspiration in light of the work you will have to do to be able to continue to substantiate it!

Sometimes it's really just about claiming something that your competitors don't claim. At the time of writing, telco BT is running a campaign that claims it is the only home wi-fi company to guarantee wi-fi in every room. It isn't particularly clever or sexy, nor as a matter of fact is it necessarily unique to them. But nobody else bothers saying it. By claiming it as their proposition they will attract almost every customer for whom a lack of signal strength at home is a concern.

To get this right you need to think about how customers think of themselves. This might fall into several categories:

- Situational
- Need to catch up (with the Joneses, or the competition, or the market)
- Wanting to change (self-image, ways of working, focus)
- Need to make things perfect
- Need to win
- Personal
- Entrepreneur

- Visionary
- Winner
- Determined
- Risk-averse

And so on.

One of the best propositions I've ever worked on was with a digital marketing agency called Impero. They looked closely at who their favourite clients were, what they enjoyed doing most and the outcomes they were most proud of. After an intensive workshop we came up with *'We make tired brands famous again.'*

They recognised that they could be the best in the world at this, because they had made waves by working with older brands that had lost their market dominance, and by applying novel thinking and great insights they had turned them around, putting them back in contention. Having done this several times previously they decided to make it a focal point. In fact, they decided to focus on this at the expense of all other work.

This meant they could focus on becoming better at brand turnarounds, and by claiming leadership they could build their experience and expertise and develop market dominance. After two years, we had doubled revenue and the agency had won five Agency of the Year awards.

The really clever thing about this proposition is that while it looks exclusive, it isn't. It appeals to any head of marketing new in post who has convinced their employer that they can turn the brand around. The reason it appeals? It directly addresses the customer's situation, implicit fears and aspirations in one stand-out phrase.

Being single-minded

The beauty of a single-minded proposition when it comes to the 2Y3X Roadmap work is that it is directive. Once a proposition has been established, assuming it meets the Hedgehog Concept definition, you know what it is you will need to do to meet the expectations of your future customers. This means focusing your product and service lines to only those that meet the passion/greatness/profit target or are required in order to deliver it.

In the industries I come from, tech startups and marketing, there is a tendency to try and be all things to all people in order not to miss out potential customers. However, casting a broad net means catching all sorts of fish you don't want or need. Far better to have customers coming to you because you're the best in the business at what you do. Think Sennheiser, Bugatti, Hunter Boots, Lidl, Burton Snowboards or Bic Biros. The best companies with the tightest propositions recognise that they can't have all the customers, and in fact most don't want to be the biggest in the world. What they want is to be brilliant, to be recognised, to make good money, to have a company people really want to work for – these are usually sufficient.

So why try and attract all the customers? It's OK to be exclusive, to qualify out some potential buyers. By polarising some people out, you will polarise other people in. These customers are likely to agree with the way you work, the standards you maintain, the ethos you have and even the core values you no longer publish on your website. They'll be more aligned with you and your people, easier to work with and keep happy, they will remain customers for longer, reducing the cost of churn, and they will also spend more.

A tight, highly attractive proposition drives growth, underpinning total team focus, decisions on specialism and training. It attracts self-identifying clients and ambitious staff. And nine times out of ten it makes your staff say, 'Oh, that's what we're going to be the best in the world at!'

Here are a couple of other proposition examples which both identify the audience's needs and define the proposition owner's ongoing business focus:

- Chatbot company Synthetic: *Conversations worth millions*
- Creative firm Hub: *Extraordinary audience engagement*
- Branding agency White Bear: *Branding for future unicorns*

If you'd like to read more about competitive differentiation and proposition development, and don't want to wait for my next book, which is on exactly this topic (though if you do, sign up for updates at ScaleAtSpeed.com), then I'd recommend *Creating Competitive Advantage* and *Good to Great* as good starting points.

Lead generation

There is a difference between cold-calling a hundred clients hoping they will meet with you, and having ten clients come to you with an established need.

One of the problems with the first approach is that some clients feel it is their job to meet new suppliers so they keep up with their market knowledge. This is why lead-generation or telesales agencies have a brilliant honeymoon but rarely produce sales: they get you meetings from their little black books with the serial meeters. It takes a miracle for you to actually call a prospect at the moment they have a specific need.

In fact, there's a cute Venn diagram (yes, another one) that describes the absolute requirements for a lead that can be readily converted:

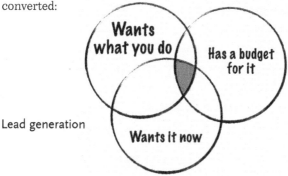

Lead generation

If they don't have a budget themselves, then they'll have to pitch someone else for it. You won't have control, and you can't win. If they don't need it right now, then pitching them is a waste of their time and yours. You'll need someone who fits all three criteria to meet the definition of a properly qualified lead. The chances of you or a telemarketer getting through to one by hitting the phones are astronomically low. You're more likely to get through to someone who shares your birthday.[12] That's why most sales people insist that it's a numbers game. If you do it their way, they're right.

A lead-generation formula needs to take into account that you are resource-light, and don't want to waste your time sending people who probably aren't senior enough to meetings you know are likely to be fruitless. You want a qualified prospect to see your company at its best, and you cannot do this by spreading yourselves too thin. So let's focus once again on our qualified lead. They want what you do, they have a budget already set aside for it, and they want it now.

The easiest, most efficient way for you to know when you've got one of these prospects is if they come to you and they qualify themselves. Here's an analogy: you're a petrol station. You position yourself by the side of the road and put up a big sign. When someone needs petrol they'll stop. You don't need to do any persuading: they identified their need, established they can pay, and that their tank's empty. Self-qualifying lead. All you have to do is be ready.

The classic attractors for self-qualifying leads are PR (speeches, articles, interviews, quotes in the press), content marketing (white papers, videos, podcasts) and events (breakfast briefings, seminars, specialist conferences). My firm puts on specialist conferences a couple of times each year. This alone brings us almost all of our new consulting clients, and this plus referrals accounts for most of the 2Y3X Programme's new clients each year.

---

[12] In a group of more than twenty-three people there is a 50 per cent likelihood that someone will share your birthday. See https://en.wikipedia.org/wiki/Birthday_problem for the maths.

Advertising and social media campaigns are also options. Provided your proposition is utterly clear, and your target audience can easily identify themselves as both being in your catchment and in need of what you're selling, they will come to you, usually exactly when they're ready. All you have to do is not screw up the pitch.

Task
Month 1 – Research

- Gather data on your customers' decision-makers and influencers, when they are most likely to buy, and what their budget will be.
- Identify a pressing need for information and its timing and role in the buying cycle.

Month 2 – Prototype

- Develop your content.
- Plan and set up the campaign.

Month 3 – Implement

- Promote the content/event.
- Measure campaign and content response rates and start to refine the plan for the next campaign.
- Run the event, if that's what you're doing, and gather feedback from all attendees so you can improve it next time.
- Begin following up all leads.
- Establish who will be responsible for this activity going forwards.

You may find that this task is too big to get finished in a single quarter. If this is the case, you will usually find out at the research phase.

That's the time when the scale issue should be flagged, and a decision made by the GLT as to whether it should be split over two successive quarters. If so, determine what the new definition of each quarterly task should be. One of the next quarter's tasks could be delayed to make way for the completion of this one – it's important to get your new business flow right as soon as possible, as this is your fuel for growth.

The basics of a weighted pipeline

In an ideal world revenue would be predictable. Most of the companies I work with have two types of income: predictable, repeating, licence-based or retainer-based; and unpredictable ad hoc or project work.

Predictable revenue comes from fixed-price contracts for long-term repeating work. Once agreed with a customer it can be perfectly predicted for a reasonable period – say a year, sometimes three years – in advance. In an ideal world this work has a very high barrier to exit that isn't just contract-based. This can come in the form of a high cost to switch, few equivalent competitors, or continuous market pressure or demand. The more of this kind of work you can win, the more stable your business is likely to be. If you could make it 100 per cent predictable then this would be ideal, although at some point almost every contract eventually comes to an end and you have to replace the revenue. Predicting the rate of success of winning replacement contracts remains extremely important.

On the other hand, while ad hoc and project-based work is welcome, it also adds uncertainty to long-range planning and unpredictability to short-term cash flow, and by extension sometimes to staff morale. While an awful lot of good customer management is about turning ad hoc customers into long-term predictable revenue streams by leveraging the CSS, often this only applies to a small percentage of your customer relationships. If you can't predict the future, you're a bit stuck. You can't plan ahead. And if your customers can't provide 100 per cent of the data you need for clairvoyance, then you need to look elsewhere.

The nearest source then is your sales pipeline.

Unfortunately, it's rare that business owners take the trouble to use their sales function to predict revenue. Usually, having enough salespeople or enough sales calls or enough pitches on is sufficient to give us a feeling for whether we're going to be busy enough. While I am all for gut feel when it comes to deal-making, I am a big, big fan of data when it comes to uncertainty. And running a business is all about managing uncertainty. Because when you manage uncertainty and start to gather data, uncertainty becomes risk. And risk is quantifiable: you can make decisions based on risk, whereas making decisions based on uncertainty is a fool's game. I described earlier how to use Bayesian Inference to help you make risky decisions. It doesn't help, however, if you have no data at all!

Your Customer Relationship Marketing system (CRM)[13] is the place to start.

Firstly, if you don't have a CRM then it's probably high time you went and got one. For a thirty-person business it will take perhaps twenty hours to set it up with all your calls, leads, prospects, deals in the making and customers, and that includes getting your head around it and making sure it's linked with your emails, website analytics, mailing lists and your other sales stakeholders. Planned right, this could be a Q-Zero task for someone on the GLT. In the meantime, a spreadsheet will do, though not really for long.

If you already have a CRM system in place, then the second thing to do is to find a way to assign a probability score to each stage of a lead's journey towards a sale. While you may have many steps to cover – from first contact to first conversation, needs discovery to sales proposal – the simplest way of developing a predictable pipeline is to assign a very simple deal likelihood score: 10 per cent, 50 per cent and 90 per cent.

---

[13] Having worked with CRM pioneer Mei Lin Fung and been CEO of a CRM strategy firm, I am aware there are several ways of defining CRM. I have used it here to denote sales CRM software.

By assigning every lead one of these three quite disparate scores it encourages salespeople (including you) not to skew the numbers too much by over-estimating the probability of a lead turning into a deal.

You also need to set a predicted close date, and monitor these against actual close dates. This way you can start to increase the accuracy of your predictions when deals close. Oh, and a quick note: closing means closing to a 'no' just as much as closing to a 'yes'. You really don't need never-gonna-happen deals hanging around confusing your numbers. As we saw in the previous section, if they don't want it now, they're not worth having in your pipeline. Though of course if you know when in the future they will 'want it now', then you can take them out of your current pipeline and add them back in at the appropriate time.

By adding in data on probability you can multiply the probability by the potential deal value for each lead to give you a weighted value; aggregating all of these weighted values will give you an overall value of your current pipeline. This value – when you are confident of its accuracy – will allow you to pre-plan your resources for the expected volume of work.

To increase your confidence in the data you therefore need to add a score for the accuracy of the last period's pipeline prediction, and tweak the formula accordingly. Barring events outside your control (which should be tracked in your SWOT and included in your risk register, covered in Chapter 7), the sales pipeline should give you confidence enough to plan ahead. Data means you can assess risks and plan for scenarios according to their likelihood. Lack of data means you have to guess. Guessing leads to feast and famine, reactive, back-foot decision-making, and sometimes bankruptcy.

Task
Month 1 – Research

- Find out how leads are recorded – spreadsheet, emails, CRM?

- Evaluate conversion rate patterns by type of customer, lead source or the approach taken to convert the lead.
- Research CRM systems for suitability to your volume of leads to customers and test one or two.

Month 2 – Prototype

- Set up the chosen CRM system.
- Integrate the CRM with your website, email marketing system, your sales email account and your contacts database.
- Populate with last six months' leads to provide a baseline for future improvements.

Month 3 – Implement

- Populate with all current leads and assign a lead score for each based on the '10 per cent, 50 per cent, 90 per cent' principle.
- Derive an overall pipeline value (all leads multiplied by the probability of each converting) and report to the GLT each month from now on. This will show the team whether the pipeline is growing or shrinking, and over time will allow you to establish a forecast-versus- reality ratio and improve it.

How to win pitches

Wouldn't it be wonderful if we could all just be order-takers? If the right customers would come to us knowing we can deliver what they want, and just give us the money and take the products or services we provide? Every business would be a cash cow. And yet even businesses where this is normally how it works need to be proactive. Your team needs to be constantly seeking out new opportunities with existing and new customers. You need to innovate to survive.

In service industries we have proposals and sales meetings. Proposals are a way for customers to compare a number of potential suppliers point-by-point, prior to having to negotiate – they are a way of keeping potential suppliers at arm's length. I dislike proposals for the simple reason that the chances of winning the business are incredibly low if you can't discuss the value you will bring to the customer, because you have no idea how many companies you're up against, no control over timing and no influence during a discussion. Proposals usually mean you're competing on price. And commodity pricing is something you might want to avoid, unless you can consistently beat your competitors on price for some reason: by controlling the supply chain, manufacturing your own products, or perhaps offshoring to suppliers where labour and materials costs are lower than where your customers are. Otherwise, sending written proposals puts you and your competitors on a more or less level playing field. When I ran my own companies I never wanted a level playing field.

Sales meetings are a way for clients to work out who they will work with, usually from a shortlist of three or five possible suppliers. You have already done the important work of allowing them to identify you, to self-qualify as wanting what you provide. You've narrowed your competitive set. Now it is time to win the business.

It's an extremely expensive business, pitching. If it takes four people a week to do all the work to win a new client, that's a month's salary. Worth it if you win every sale. Not worth it if one in three means winning only four per year. So, if you can find a way of winning without pitching at all – which is what these chapters on positioning and lead generation are about – then pursue it. And if you can, win the majority of pitches you're forced to do by making the pitch process itself work in your favour ...

The next section focuses on a deeply rational, logical method that uncovers hidden value and insights and turns you into the customer's business partner. The section after that focuses on the irrational, using the lizard brain to get deals to close themselves. The combination of the two is incredibly powerful.

Value-based selling

For you to sell products or services at a high price, the customer needs to understand the value of what they are buying. Sometimes the value is based on implicit assumptions about status – more expensive must mean higher quality, more famous must mean higher trust, etc.

These are attitudes that are extremely long in the making, and usually take hold by osmosis over many years. If you are trying to sell a premium-priced product or service, you are unlikely to have the time to convince someone who doesn't already have these attitudes. I realised this years ago when I ran the world's most-awarded web design firm. You will not persuade a client who is used to advertising sofas with 20 per cent-off sales stickers that elegant design values will produce better returns. They either already know it or they don't believe it or they have satisfactorily proven their own viewpoint.

Some assumptions and positions about value are already present in the buyer.

You need an approach that bypasses these assumptions and digs into what's actually valued by the customer, so you can present your solution to their need in such a way that they can see and recognise – in their own terms – that you can deliver the value they require. In order for you to meet the 'on their own terms' requirement, you need to find a way to get them to define to you what's valuable to them. Otherwise you need to be a mind reader, and although it's on the job scorecard for most salespeople, the reality is that as entrepreneurs you need to be the lead evangelist and salesperson for your company until such time as you can hire telepaths to take over from you.

One methodology offers a solution. It's derived from Neil Rackham's *SPIN Selling*, which is one of those sales methods that all diligent enterprise salespeople will read, but is far too formulaic for the non-professional to learn and practise. I have a simplified version that can be used in almost any situation, but first I'll set the scene.

'It started off so well. The client called us in for a meeting so we could present our credentials and see if we'd get on. The meeting was brilliant, our slides rocked, and the chemistry was amazing. They loved us. I even arranged to go for beers with the guy once the selection process was over.'

'So what happened at the pitch?'

'We did the usual brilliant job of coming up with a plan to meet their brief. In fact, we went above and beyond: we came up with three fantastic solutions to their problem. We even checked in with them a few days before the pitch to make sure the solutions were on track. I had Adam re-check our pitch against their brief line by line to make sure we'd answered every requirement in detail . . .'

'. . . and?'

'When we got in the room all that great chemistry seemed to have gone. There were another couple of people in the room on their side, which we expected, but they just didn't seem to remember how well we'd got on. They told us at the end that they thought our solutions would definitely work, so I was hopeful, but then they called and told me we came a close second. Sorry, Jo, not sure what happened.'

Familiar? This seems to be the norm for almost every company I've worked with, including in the early days my own. So what happened in this situation? What went wrong?

Imagine, if you will, there are three companies pitching for the same contract. Each has a charismatic leader or salesperson. All the people who are sent to the creds meeting are presentable, sane and personable. Everyone in the room is trying their best to be likeable. The chemistry is always going to be great. That's a level playing field. You have, thus far, a one-in-three chance of winning.

It is worth remembering that the client has already seen everyone's credentials. They've already been on the website, read the white papers, looked at other examples of work, asked around, perhaps even spoken with a client or two. Yet your salesperson spent an hour in a meeting being charming and telling the client team a bunch of stuff they already knew. The buyers must have been bored out of their minds. One of your competitors did exactly the same thing. The remaining competitor did something different.

Your rival's salesperson, let's call her Alice, spent five minutes being charming and engaging everyone in the room, reminding the client's team that they wouldn't have invited her company in if they didn't already know what they did and the level of quality they produce. Instead of spending an hour showing slide after slide, she simply told those present that her company had recently produced a million in new profits for another customer, but to do so she had to ask some questions. So she started asking the client her questions.

'Your brief asks us to increase the number of visitors to your stores by 10 per cent. How many people is that?'

'What does a 10 per cent increase mean in terms of additional sales revenue?'

'What's the conversion rate you currently get from visitors to purchasers?'

'What's the conversion variation between your highest and lowest performing stores?'

'If you could identify locations where it was easy to increase conversion versus those where it's impossible, would that be valuable?'

For the sake of this illustration I'll pause here. Alice's questions are about uncovering value, in terms of both immediate dollars and more removed return on investment.

'Your brief asks us to increase the number of visitors to your stores by 10 per cent. How many people is that?'

This is simply a ranging question. It gives us information that we can later use to make the commercial solution more human rather than just about numbers and percentages. However, it's really the numbers that count here.

'What does a 10 per cent increase mean in terms of additional sales revenue?'

This gives us a dollar figure. We now know what the revenue per visitor is, and can base ROI calculations on this. We also know what the client needs us to deliver in revenue terms as a baseline, and we can gauge their required ROI on this by comparing their stated budget with the required return.

'What's the conversion rate you currently get from visitors to purchasers?'

This gives us revenue per purchaser. It also gives us an idea of what improvements we might make by focusing on where visitors could be converted better.

'What is the lifetime value of a customer?'

Simple, but useful to know.

'What's the conversion variation between your highest and lowest performing stores?'

This gives us an idea of the range of opportunity and scope for identifying highest ROI by store (and if we dig deep enough, the numbers we could expect to see).

'If you could identify locations where it was easy to increase conversion versus those where it's impossible, would that be valuable?'

This is where our strategy starts to become clear: we are interested here in delivering value to our client, not just footfall. Alice is uncovering what the client perceives has value to their eyes.

The questioning session is there to identify quantifiable outcomes. Each question either builds on the last, or adds to the pool of outcomes. These outcomes can then be used to work out what value the required service has, both in immediate simple terms and in a variety of longer-term or wider contexts. (By the way, if the data on the first question or two can be obtained through background research, then you validate your understanding with your client and move on.)

Why do you want to know this? Because a brief for a supplier is the result of a long chain of decisions, each of which has got progressively smaller until the output was an email to your office and a briefing document. As such, in order to deliver all the value that a brief can possibly imply, you need to move progressively up the chain of value. In an ideal world, a notional Question 17 would be, 'What would a $20 million cost saving do to your share price?' This may be beyond your scope and well beyond the pay grade of the client decision-maker, but ultimately that's what the CEO is really looking for.

So, you need to ask these questions. Question 1 = Answer 1 = Value 1; Question 2 = Answer 2 = Value 2 and so on. Then Alice goes back to the office.

Here is where the fundamental difference in the pitch happens. Alice's team are not just thinking about Answer 1, which your salesperson and the other competitor are focusing on. They're thinking about Answer 1 in the context of Value 1, Value 2, Value 3, Value 4 and Value 5. In fact, they have come up with the insight that if there were a cost-effective sales training programme, in-store conversions might double, and, based on the numbers established in other answers, the overall results of the campaign would be doubled to 20 per cent at a training cost of 2 per cent. That's a staggeringly different result than your salesperson would be able to promise.

Questioning numbers always leads to more numbers, as opposed to questioning intangibles, which tends always to lead to the relative dead end of the client team's personal goals. This is, after all, business.

You need to focus on it. You can look after psychology using different sales tools which I'll cover in the next section.

By looking at all the numbers, you will gain insights. Insights lead to solutions that aren't just one-dimensional, but take into account the client's overall business needs. What you are doing is identifying just what this project could mean for the client if they got it right.

And that becomes the pitch.

On pitch day, Alice presents the numbers, their implications, the financial consequences if those issues are addressed. What she is showing is that rather than just the 10 per cent more footfall, this solution will deliver 18 per cent (once training has been costed in); that this can be increased further by focusing on customer lifetime value once a customer has converted; that by focusing budgets on segments and stores that are most likely to rise, we are saving money and refocusing it where it will produce the greatest ROI. She's even showing that when it comes to new store openings, the locations should be similar to the easily expanded, not the hard-to-expand.

She finishes the pitch with the final number, the big one with the millions after it, as the total value delivered. Alice has shown she understands what the stakes are of getting this wrong, and the rewards of getting it right. She understands the client's business requirements, not just the brief's.

Your firm comes second to Alice's in the pitch – though we all know every loser is always told they were a close second simply out of politeness, but in fact you weren't even close.

You weren't even on the same playing field.

The interesting thing is that this method applies to selling in almost any industry, including, for example, manufacturing:

'Your Request for Proposal (RFP) specifies bearings with a minimum life of X – what sits behind that requirement?'

'So they have to have a minimum lifecycle of two years. What is the

cost of replacing bearings in this system?'

'And for every hour of downtime, what does that cost in terms of unused labour?'

'And what is the cost in terms of lost production?'

'Are there any other consequential costs like the costs of transportation delays?'

And so on. Instead of writing a proposal that focuses on the precise specifications of the bearings you're going to supply, how quickly they can be supplied and their commodity cost, you can point out why a slightly more expensive type of bearing will ultimately save the company millions in lost revenue and opportunity costs. You might also add in a maintenance or telemetry service, thereby adding significant revenue to your sale while still saving your customer time, convenience and real money. This is why this sales method is all about value and not price.

After I started practising it I found this method of pitching to be fascinating. On the one hand it's easy to wing the questioning, especially if you have had some good training in coaching. On the other hand, when you really prepare your questions well, the figures you uncover can be quite remarkable. Experience will give you the questions that are relevant to your prospects and clients (and clients you already work with can provide much insight here), but – assuming you do some research into your prospects before you meet them for the first time – a bank of prepared questions will never be a waste of time.

One thing that happened straight away for the companies I introduced this to: they all stopped using credentials decks (interminable boilerplate 'who-we-are' slide presentations). I haven't used a creds deck in ten years. I just introduce myself, explain that I get results by asking questions, and dive in. The startups, consultancies, agencies and tech firms I've worked with combine strong positioning with value-based selling and win 70 per cent of their pitches.

There's a secondary application that is really useful too. You can use this method within an existing client relationship, in which case the conversation can become a consequent-value conversation. A little bit of digging and uncovering, some thoughtful questions about what it would mean if x – this kind of dialogue can be initiated by anyone from a product owner or project manager to an account executive. The intel you will acquire by building this into your developing relationships with your clients will allow you to uncover the real stakes for them. You will come up with more proactive proposals, suggest ways to save as well as make money, and become their business partner (difficult to replace), not just their supplier (all too easy to replace). This increases your own customers' lifetime value, reduces the number of pitches you must do to replace lost clients and means you can focus on more profitable and faster growth.

Finally, this method gives you tacit permission to ask for unusually deep results data so you can monitor the effects and consequent effects of the services you provide. In turn, this gives you results that will attract other, similar clients. Your competitors will wonder how you can produce such big results from such a small brief.

Psychology in sales

We've just seen how the content of a pitch or proposal can sharply differentiate you from your competitors.

However, it's often the case that, no matter how good your pitch, you simply can't seem to close deals. I wanted to look at a few things that commonly hold businesses back – no matter how good the content – from winning customers.

One thing that comes up time and again is confidence.

You go into the sales meeting fully prepared, well-rehearsed (ahem, I say that, but lots of business owners never rehearse, because they believe their passion will get them through. Have you ever been asked who your other customers are, and your mind goes blank? That's down to rehearsal, or the lack of it), and you still somehow feel like you're on the back foot in front of the client.

Believe it or not, many buyers are trained in deliberately putting potential suppliers on the defensive. Evil though it may be, it puts the power in the hands of the buyer, and that is where beating you down on costs comes in. Here are a few examples of how a potential buyer can unsettle the potential supplier (you):

- Keeping you cooling your heels in a soulless reception
- Keeping you waiting in an ostentatiously large (yet strangely uncomfortable) reception
- Making you wait in chairs that are peculiarly low and a struggle to get up from
- Making you wait a while before the meeting, even though you turned up on time
- Sitting in a row behind a table facing the door as you enter the room, interview-style
- The senior decision-maker turning up late and asking you to be quick, or, worse, telling you that you only have half the time arranged
- Telling you at the last minute that you have a large number of competitors willing to do better on price.

Strangely familiar? All these are tactics to make you feel you have to compete for the buyer's order. It puts all the power in the relationship on them. All the pricing power. In business it is, I'm afraid, the politics of fear in action.

The usual answer is to remember they put their pants on one leg at a time (a maxim that works oddly well in both British and American English). However, in this case I prefer to be a little more dogmatic than pragmatic. You need to remember that they need you as much as you want them.

They would not be running a pitch for new suppliers unless they had to. If their current supplier were any good, they wouldn't be moving. If they were paying the right price for the value derived, they wouldn't be moving. If they didn't have to, they wouldn't be moving. Your opportunity is their mandatory.

There's a classic joke about two men out hunting who disturb a bear, which then gives chase. 'It's hopeless,' says one, 'we can't outrun the bear!'

'I don't have to outrun the bear,' calls the other, sprinting ahead. 'I only have to outrun you!'

You don't have to compete with the buyer, your prospect. You only have to outclass your competitors. Which you'll be doing with the value you deliver. This means you should not pay heed to the customer's attempts to undermine your confidence in order to gain a spurious upper hand. Your job is to meet them as partners, having left your competitors behind.

The problem is, once you surrender, there's no way back. So the second someone starts to play power games you should back off, or meet them head on. If the lead decision-maker can't make the meeting at the last moment, rearrange it. It is infinitely better to lose some travelling time than your ability to negotiate a fair price – you will forever be beholden to them, whether they want you to drop everything to supply something overnight, or at lower cost, or at the cost of your other customers' satisfaction and wellbeing.

We discussed value in terms of what the customer will get when they work with you. That's what this is all about: everyone having fair value. You have just as much value as the prospective customer: you want a fair exchange of the value your service or product can deliver for the value of their cash.

Have this firmly in mind: you are just as much the prize to them – given how much more valuable you are than your competitors – as their budget is to you.

By thinking like this on your way into every sales situation you can have a conversation grown-up to grown-up about the things each side is looking for, and how to match it to the available purse. You'll come unstuck if you go down the route of trying to come up with 'added value extras', because surely if both sides of the negotiation table were really equally prized then one would expect the customer to do the same.

Which leads neatly into premium pricing. If you can truly differentiate your proposition, products or services from your competitors in value terms then you should be able to command higher prices. And if you can genuinely demonstrate greater value (and there is a market for premium products or services), then you will have those higher prices paid. In my own experience, the higher your prices, the more likely the prospect will assume your prices are worth it. There's plenty of research into pricing strategies, but at a rudimentary level if you charge twice as much as others people will assume you're significantly better; and the more you charge the more they will value the service or products they receive, and the more they value it the more they will appreciate it and try to keep the relationship in balance (as opposed to trying to maintain a power dynamic that can only end in one side's frustration and possible failure).

Remember: you are just as important, necessary and valuable as your prospective customer, and you will find the whole process easier and less soul-destroying. Your salespeople will be happier, your confidence will be much, much higher, and you will win more often. Be the charismatic prize and clients will fall at your feet.

A few psychological tricks that may also come in useful:

• All of us are motivated primarily by fear. Consequently, your proposals should first be mindful of the fears the buyer may harbour. More on this in the next chapter.
• We are hardwired to chase things that are moving away from us. Any sale will be easier to close (to either a no or a yes, doesn't matter which) if there is a hard deadline, preferably

imposed by the market or some external force. Though to be honest it can be as artificial as you like – 'Sale ends Monday!' still works on you even though you're smart as a whip.

• We are hardwired to want what we can't have. 'We have this product but we're not sure you're going to be able to afford it' is a surprisingly effective sales argument.

Finally, a majorly important top tip when selling: *don't be afraid of telling your prospect the price.* If you go into a presentation about the value of your product or service, and the value is higher than the price, then it's a no-brainer. If it's equal to the price, it's fair. If the price is higher than the value, then you're going to lose the sale – also common sense. This applies whether it's pitching a major consultancy project or to build a motorway, or simply selling a Mars bar.

So the price only becomes worrisome if you don't believe you're worth what the sticker says.

If you're not worried about it, then you can come out and say it. My favourite thing to do in a pitch is to start the ball rolling by telling the prospect what we're going to address in the meeting, and the price of it. After that we go into detail.

'Really glad to be here today. We've done a great deal of thinking about how we can help solve your problem. We've come up with a solution which costs £100,000, and that will mean you're catered to for the next three years, while saving you £2 million. Shall I explain?'

That way you've dealt with the price right at the start of the meeting. None of this, 'If they ask the price it's a buying signal' rubbish. That's why you see the price on every car on the garage forecourt. Price up front on the sticker, then you can discuss the value of the solution. It's either worth it or not. And if they can't afford it to begin with then you can't sell to them and everyone can stop wasting each other's time. In a kind of mirror-image of the self-qualifying prospect we discussed in the section on lead generation, here you give the customer the opportunity to self-disqualify. Again, it's about having equal-to-equal discussions about how to cater to a specific need a customer has, where nobody is wasting anyone else's precious time and everyone is agreed on the frame of reference.

Some observations from the other side of the pitch table

A career spanning twenty-two years has meant over £20 million of direct sales of professional services to board-level buying teams. Often this required a team of well-prepared supplier-side folks, with a brilliantly structured pitch, awesome creative and competition-destroying secret sauce.

My teams were good, usually some of the best in the business. They were well-practised, had great rapport with each other and knew how to build it with buying teams, and had gone through some of the best sales training available. I loved the pitch process, the adrenaline and the win.

Yet it wasn't until I had finished my career as a serial founder and CEO that I experienced running a pitch as the client, sitting on the other side of the table with my board-level colleagues with a beauty parade of suppliers queued up during a long couple of days to pitch us for our business. I'd been hired as a consultant to evaluate an investment firm's marketing. The new marketing strategy had taken me three months to build. Much of that time was spent bringing the senior team up to speed in marketing best practice. The proposed numbers looked entirely sound, and quickly it came time to select some new suppliers – a web design firm, a brand expert, a content marketing agency, a media strategy consultancy and a CRM supplier. We held a pitch. I selected the vendors, briefed them, and arranged the pitch days.

Here's what was shocking. With almost a quarter-century of experience coming up with marketing strategies for companies like Procter & Gamble, Unilever, Mars, Sony and any number of Virgin brands, confidence in the strategy was never going to be an issue. Yet on the first day, walking into the boardroom, I found I was terrified. My primal, lizard brain was completely in control. I was scared.

Here's what I concluded about the process and what had affected me so unexpectedly: I was worried that the vendors would embarrass me in front of the team I had spent three months working with to convince them that the new strategy was imperative and persuade them to part with £1 million to execute it.

This came to a head when it came time for pitch day – the day when I would be sat alongside all of my colleagues, peers and bosses, listening to suppliers tell us how they would supply what we had asked for. The fear was that one or more would make themselves look stupid (making my judgement look suspect), or make me look stupid by telling the team the brief was wrong and they had a better solution. Bearing in mind I had got my colleagues to sign off on my solution as being the correct thing to do, this latter would have been catastrophic.

This insight was a total revelation to me. As an experienced and successful pitcher, I now understood for the first time what it was like to be the pitchee.

What I wanted, as the client, was for each vendor to tell us how they would deliver what we had asked for better than their competitors. Not to tell us what we had asked for was wrong. If they had come up with a better idea, then I wanted them to have talked it through with me before the pitch, so I could either shoot it down fast or make sure it landed with the rest of the team. If it was a better idea, then cool, let me help get it through – but please, please do not under *any* circumstances catch me on the back foot or embarrass me in front of my colleagues.

This revelation – that base instinct and uncontrolled emotion would rise up unexpectedly to colour my decision-making – led me to re-evaluate pitching and sales methodologies altogether. I eventually found a book called *Pitch Anything* by Oren Klaff, which focuses solely on how to make use of this lizard brain to formulate and win pitches. It is, I think, the single best book on selling I have read, because it focuses not on the processes but on the motivations that drive the decision.

Sales training is one of the crucial components of almost every roadmap I have ever helped construct. Whether it is delivered by one of the great sales training companies over several weeks or months, or done one workshop at a time led by an experienced non-exec or internal sales trainer, it doesn't matter. What is important is that it is done regularly, and with the marketing, sales and usual new business teams as well as account handlers, those responsible for repeat selling, cross-selling and up-selling existing clients, and those responsible for dealing with customer complaints. A good place to start sales training is with the growth lab team.

KEY TAKEAWAYS

- Many businesses fall victim to 'feast and famine' cycles, where marketing, prospecting, selling and onboarding take turns, leaving you vulnerable to market or business cycle shifts. Continuous processes mitigate these risks to your survival.
- Your proposition must be single-minded, make your company stand out from your competitive field, be memorable and resonate with the buyer's world view. A great proposition will attract customers to you.
- Reach new customers by teaching them about what you do. It will establish your expertise in their eyes.
- Sell value: identify both the positive contribution and money/time/effort savings your product or service offers. Focus on this to escape the commodification trap and provide opportunities to sell more to existing customers.
- Don't forget that your customer is human, too.

6

Financial and Corporate

Leaky buckets

It is critical that you're not turning on the tap to fill a leaky bucket. All the new sales in the world mean nothing in the end if you are not profitable, and if you don't have the stability to weather storms. This chapter addresses the essentials, and a later section in Chapter 8 shows you a way to teach the fundamentals to your GLT.

For the longest time I didn't understand finances at all. In fact, at my first couple of companies I'm not sure anyone did. Then one of my competitors told me about spreadsheets, and a light bulb went on in my brain. For many years I kept a cash flow spreadsheet that I designed, using lots of colours to make it pretty so I'd be able to follow it. This saved my bacon over and over again – my ability to model what was coming up meant I could juggle payments accordingly and squeak through several nasty incidents where a major client left, or someone didn't pay, or we had to move office and find a cash deposit. What I failed to realise was that just having a handle on cash flow wasn't enough; if I focused on making a profit the cash would start to sort itself out, and eventually I wouldn't have to worry about it quite so obsessively.

It took a patient finance director (and eventual investor in one of my companies) to teach me how a profit & loss (P&L) works, and how to read a balance sheet. This gave me wings, and was the start of my real business career. Had I understood basic finances I am certain I would have been much more successful much earlier. Though I probably wouldn't have written this book. My excuse is that I was too busy trying to change the world, and had neglected to consider adding a financial KPI to my list of goals.

You too probably have too many responsibilities competing for your attention. And when times are unpredictable, competition from the outside adds yet more pressure. Good financial governance delivers profit, cash, reserves – and safety.

So how do you create this safety?

Customers love survivors. I don't mean people who've had long careers: I mean companies that are well run. Built to last. Prepared for all the ups and downs in a shifting and unpredictable economy and rapidly changing consumer landscape.

Customers want – no, they need – to know their suppliers are in great shape. Why? Because it's a costly business changing supplier: a failing relationship produces distracted work that generates less value; running a pitch costs scarce management time; and onboarding a new relationship may mean months before sales pick up again. The risk to the customer of a critical supplier that falls over after being hired is not one many are prepared to take.

Aside from being brilliant, the ideal company needs a decent balance sheet. This provides a robust safety net. It gives agency managers the flexibility to work with unpredictable customers, do rush projects, move into new disciplines based on customer demand, cope when there's a lull in sales, and make brilliant hires when the opportunity arises. It also allows you to be tactical about acquisitions, especially in tougher times when competitors without the resources to be flexible might struggle. A strong balance sheet gives you power.

A strong balance sheet, in practical terms, means having at least three times your monthly staff costs and overheads – what it costs in total to run your business – in the bank. Before the COVID-19 crisis it was often good enough for some of this to be in the debtor book, but when customers stopped paying overnight at the same time as companies desperately needed their reserves, this changed.

With this in mind, it's imperative that your company is run as a cash-generative business. You should be delivering a good 20 per cent net profit (a year of which gives you your safe minimum of three months' costs in the bank), and it needs to be fairly consistent so you are constantly building reserves, which you can then use for future growth.

Twenty per cent takes determination. To quote the Eisenberg brothers' wonderful book, *Be Like Amazon: Even a Lemonade Stand Can Do It*, 'It's simple but not easy.' However, once you've made the changes outlined here it becomes much easier to maintain.

And guess what? Customers want to work with you because you're determined, and have vision and a clear belief in what you're doing. You have strength and resilience when times are tough, and flexibility and nimbleness when clients need tactical. In your team you build confidence. Against your peers you can be fearless.

Collecting the money you're owed

Once upon a time, I ran my company hand-to-mouth. I'm hoping this isn't familiar to you, but the reality is it probably is. There were frequently times when I wasn't really sure we had enough cash to cover all our bills and salaries at the end of the month. As founders, it was always of course my partner and I who got paid last. Occasionally we had to dip our hands into our pockets to make sure someone else got paid.

I absolutely loathed that situation. Even as I write now it's made me a bit stressed and retrospectively resentful just thinking about it. Incidentally, stress mostly comes from situations that are outside your control. Most of the business stresses I faced as a naive entrepreneur felt way out of my control. I bet your stresses come from the same things. Staff leaving out of the blue. Clients behaving unpredictably. Servers going down. Suppliers flaking out. Not enough pitches on when you really need it. Being beaten by the competition time after time.

Yet, as we've seen throughout this book, most of these things can be brought under control. Not by being reactive. You can't wrangle a company's fortunes into submission by attacking every problem as it arises, by being the best solver or crisis manager in the business. You remove these sources of ulcers and sleepless nights by preventing them occurring in the first place. You make this place a wonderful place to work because everyone's values are aligned and the work is satisfying. You predict client needs by monitoring their sentiment and satisfaction and by identifying their need for value well in advance. You vet your staff and your suppliers to minimise the risk that they will flake out. And you avoid a critical lack of new business by monitoring your pipeline and reacting instantly when pre-emptive action is required.

Recently our web server did go down at a critical moment. There's little you can do about that particular stress other than try to remain polite and pragmatic, and refer to your risk register (more on that in a bit). Pretty much everything else can be prevented by having a well set-up company.

Pre-emption also applies to cash collection or credit control. Credit control is one of those phrases that feels like jargon, but done properly does what it says on the tin: it's about controlling the credit lines you give to your customers if you don't get the money up front (e.g. in a shop or via e-commerce). We forget, way too often, that we give our customers credit to buy our services. We loan them our services in the expectation they will pay later. It's the same whether you're an ad agency, a restaurant, a cleaner or a taxi driver. We deliver the goods, then we get paid, because we assume the customer is trustworthy.

With this in mind, in order for the customer to remain in our good books they need to pay on time. Logic says if they pay late they are demonstrably not trustworthy enough to be given credit.

Think about that.

And if they pay you a month late, that's a month's cash you don't have available to you to run your business – you've lent it to someone who has failed to pay it back on time!

If your usual terms of business are to offer thirty days' credit terms, and yet on average you collect your money into your bank after sixty days, that's 8.3 per cent of your entire turnover you don't have at your disposal. If your revenue is three million, that's a quarter of a million missing from your bank account. That's a third of your safety net. Or a quarter of a million you could be spending on marketing and lead generation. Or a quarter of a million to acquire a critical supplier. Or a quarter of a million to launch into a new territory. That's a huge amount of money. That's sitting in your disrespectful customer's bank account earning them aggregated interest income that isn't even a rounding error to their CEO.

If you didn't pay your shopkeeper at the till or cab driver at the end of your journey, they'd be very unlikely to take more work from you unless you paid up in advance. So why should you tolerate your customers treating you with similar contempt? Well, you shouldn't. We're all guilty of forgetting that this is a simple business transaction (this deliverable for that amount of money) with some simple rules (your agreed credit terms).

This is another reminder that, as we saw when discussing how to sell, you are just as good as your customer: that this is a transaction between equals who wish to exchange one thing of value for another.

Yet clients and customers often pay you late. This disrespect is intolerable. But once it has happened it is unsolvable. So as with all the other barriers to rapid growth you must act pre-emptively.

Here is a simple plan of action:

1. When you sign your contract with your customer, highlight your credit terms right up front and in bold. If they want to negotiate them and you are willing, now is the time to do it, not later when you're begging them to pay their outstanding bills so you can pay your salary.

2. At the same time, highlight the penalties for not paying on time. This should include late payment fee, interest and collection fees. List these as specific costs. If your customer intends to pay on

time (see point 1 above) then they should be happy to sign up to this. If not, then find out why, and if necessary renegotiate the credit period.

3. When you are near to invoicing your customer send a pro forma invoice to your customer's accounts department to warn them that they should expect a formal invoice to arrive on a certain date, and to remind them of the terms of credit they have signed up to.

4. On all your invoices, state the terms of credit and state in bold who signed the contract.

5. On all your invoices state the late payment penalties.

6. On the date of issue of the invoice, have your accounts department call their accounts department, email the invoice while on the phone and get them to acknowledge receipt of the invoice by email there and then. If you can't do that, use an email programme or the email functionality of a CRM application to confirm when an email has been opened and the invoice downloaded. Ideally use Xero (or similar) so you can see when the recipient actually received the invoice.

7. Seven days prior to the due date, send an email to the customer reminding them when the payment is due and checking they are able to pay it. This should highlight any issues you might need to address before any delay rather than it come as a surprise when you don't receive your funds.

8. On receipt of the funds, make sure that your accounts department calls or writes to their accounts department and says thank you. They are human beings, remember, and there is no harm in being nice and polite.

Above all, remember that their accounts department is probably being chased all the time for overdue payments. You being nice, and reminding them in advance of what needs doing when, and making their lives really easy, will ensure you're on the top of the pile every time it comes to invoice payments day.

Credit control feeds one of the company's financial KPIs: *Average debtor days*. This is the number of days after you submit your invoice that the money turns up in your account, averaged across all payments. Credit terms should be set at around thirty days maximum – seven ideally (my consulting firm offers seven days' credit). If it gets to sixty you're wasting a month's worth of cash that could be working harder for you. This KPI can be used to manage staff who are responsible for credit control, and can (and should) become part of their job scorecard.

Critical tasks

The financial and corporate segment of the Strategy Map feels perhaps the most strategic. And yet it should really be just like every other area – strategically important, and sometimes critical in order to be able to deliver the strategic goals of the company, but otherwise just tasks and projects that serve the greater goals.

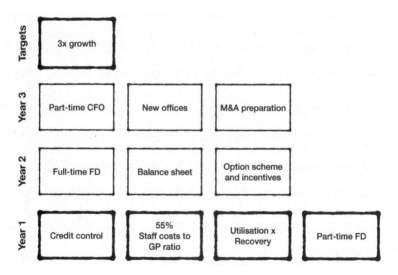

Roadmap: Finance and corporate

It is useful to break the financial targets down into end-of-year goals. Year 3's is the main financial goal, plus perhaps the numbers that feed it; for example, if the goal is three million net profit at 20 per cent of revenue, it is worth noting either the profit percentage or the overall gross profit that delivers the net profit goal. Year 2's will be two-thirds of the difference between last year and the Year 3 goal; Year 1's is this year's goal.

Important stepping stones for non-organic growth will also appear. One of our clients wanted to raise almost a million dollars for strategic acquisitions in Year 1, and to have identified four target companies. By Year 2 their target included the acquisition of three companies in two countries, and identifying opportunities to broaden their most profitable activity by doing a second acquisition in each country the following year.

So it's easy to see that if these activities are required to achieve an ambitious financial target which might not be possible to reach through organic expansion, M&A as a new business activity will in turn require new training, expertise (potentially through new hires), research and travel, financing and management. The impact must be seen in the context of all the other focus areas and vice versa: it may mean, as in the case of our client, that the CEO has to excuse him- or herself from the day-to-day management of the existing company, promote their number two, and create a separate roadmap for him- or herself.

Within the financial focus area also sits the likely resource requirement, especially in Year 2 and beyond. As a company rapidly grows through the creation of robust processes and scalable scaffolding, the more focus financial management must get. This is likely to include dedicated resources for credit control, bookkeeping, financial control, and eventually more and more input from an experienced finance director or chief finance officer – especially if M&A activity or expansion into new territories are on the cards.

Roadmap examples

Again, some of these feed into or are fed by process tasks, and the outcomes of the first three Year 1 tasks will inform future reports presented to the growth lab each month.

I would strongly encourage all business owners to bring in an external financial consultant with direct experience in your own industry to look over how your financial data is collected and reported. You may well find that there is room for optimisation, and often there are easier ways to manage your finances, especially if your finance person has grown up with your business with little prior experience at a senior level.

The rest of this chapter focuses on two critical metrics, which form two of the central KPIs for any company that wishes to grow: 'staff costs to GP ratio' and 'utilisation x recovery = efficiency'.

The magic KPI: staff costs to gross profit ratio

In the previous diagram you will have noticed the ratio of 55 per cent staff costs (which includes bonuses, dividends, taxes, pensions and so on) to gross profit.

This is a magic number. In my view it is the single most important KPI. Why? Because it is a barometer of the health of the organisation, and acts as the canary in the coal mine for staff happiness and client satisfaction. 55 per cent is the ratio that works fairly universally for services businesses – but for other sectors it might be different. You will need to identify the ratio that works best for you, of course, but I will use this particular number to illustrate the point.

First, this number more or less guarantees a net profit of 20 per cent, assuming overheads are under control and more or less fixed at 25 per cent of the gross profit of the company. It is difficult, for example, to scale rent up or down quickly (unless you rent office space by the desk, which is probably an extremely expensive way to do things). So unlike overheads, staff costs are flexible – in other words, you can easily let staff go if they are not being used or hire more if you win more work (obviously this may come with a time lag, but it is essentially true). And as we've discussed, 20 per cent net profit puts a nice buffer in the bank and gives us headroom to scale up.

Secondly, it is a gauge of how hard people are working. Assuming we are measuring *utilisation* (the number of hours a person spends on paying work for a customer) and *recovery* (how many of those utilised hours have actually been paid for by a customer) correctly, then variations up or down from 55 per cent tell us whether we are:

1. Over- or under-working staff
2. Over- or under-paying staff
3. Over- or under-billing customers
4. Over- or under-servicing customers

It is, therefore, central to understanding what changes you may need to make in hiring, remuneration, pricing or resource allocation. It also gives you a quick temperature reading of the likely morale in the wider team. If the number drops to 52 per cent and you can see that staff are working ten-hour days for a month, then you should plan for some kind of recognition of the additional effort – a night out, tactical bonuses, days off in lieu, etc. Of course, you should also adjust staffing levels so it doesn't go on too long.

Conversely, if it rises to 60 per cent, then it is likely there is either not enough work on and too many staff, or you're under-servicing your customers. Idle hands can be troublemakers; under-serviced or over-charged customers leave.

Getting your company on track quickly can be done through a quarterly task which will furnish you with both the KPI and a way of reporting it, as well as a simple plan of action for future resource management.

Task
Month 1 – Research

- Establish the current staff costs to gross profit ratio.
- Check if there is any relationship between the ratio and the current state of the company, in terms of busyness, over- (or under-) servicing of customers, and staff morale.
- Check if there is any relationship between the above and how much work is outsourced to freelancers or temporary staff.
- Check if there is any relationship between all the above and customer satisfaction.

Month 2 – Prototype

- Create a plan of action to bring the staff costs to gross profit ratio back to 55 per cent (or your equivalent).
- Develop some means of monitoring the ratio of internal versus external resources so that you can balance them better to reach the required ratio.

Month 3 – Implement

- Implement your plan.
- Inform staff and customers if necessary to give you breathing space.

This is one of those tasks that references how you monitor your staff's time per customer, your efficiency, your resource-planning capabilities and your staff's morale. It's frequently taken on as a simple KPI reporting task by the finance director, often outside the list of quarterly roadmap tasks – but eventually most internal tasks will have an impact on, and be impacted by, the staff costs-to-GP ratio.

Utilisation x recovery

Another of the KPIs we use has a strong relationship to the staff costs-to-gross profit ratio. Utilisation x recovery essentially tells us how efficient we are. The formula builds on some work that needs to be done behind the scenes to establish how much billable work each employee should be doing on average every day. Here's the formula:

Utilisation percentage x *Recovery percentage = Efficiency percentage*

Utilisation unpacked

For any given job role, how many hours per month are available for work that can be billed to a client? And of these available hours, how many were actually spent on work that can be billed to a client?

Bear in mind that any given role's day will have several components, including:

- Downtime (personal calls, fetching coffee, water cooler conversations, checking messages)
- Internal meetings (daily team huddle, weekly team meeting, all-company meetings, one-to-ones, reviews)
- Professional development (coaching, reading, learning, external training)
- Administration (reports, timesheets, filing, general resourcing, HR)
- Billable client work

At best you could expect a purely production-focused employee to spend six hours of an eight-hour day on billable work. For managers this number goes down. For senior managers it may be zero.

As you will have realised, despite each role having potentially very different numbers of available billable hours, utilisation is the measure of the percentage of those hours used for work that clients should be paying for. As such, all we need to do is add up the total of all available billable hours and, by analysing timesheet entries, work out the overall billable percentage.

For our purposes we need focus only on the percentage of the available hours actually used. With our six-productive-hours colleague, if they deliver five-and-a-half hours of billable work, their percentage utilisation is (rounded to the nearest whole number) 92 per cent.

Ideally we want this to be 100 per cent, so we will need to analyse where the time was used and adjust the balance accordingly. In other words: manage them, or encourage them to manage themselves, better. You will probably have to tweak and hone the number of billable hours set for each role as you go, based on observed data, but pretty quickly you will have roughly the right billable hours by role throughout the business. This is a task you should delegate: once the initial work has been done in the 2Y3X Roadmap to set up timesheets and reporting, refining role-specific metrics should be a job for the department heads and managers.

Why not have an average or blended billable hours metric?

While it might make sense in a steady-state company (where there is no growth), when the business is growing or shrinking it is important to have a role-based measure.

A company of, say, twenty-five staff might have six that are never billable (CEO, head of operations, admin assistant, bookkeeper, head of IT, marketing person). Blending the rate starts to go wrong as the company becomes thirty people, because it is unlikely that the number of non-billable staff will increase proportionally. Likewise, as you grow further, different departments may have to scale at entirely different rates. So the best way to do this is to define average billable hours by role (manager or non-manager) and department or discipline (production, project management, account management, planning, etc.).

For hybrid roles (for example, account managers also involved in sales), create a new client called 'Sales and Marketing' and let them allocate time to this in the timesheet system. This keeps their role scorecard simple, and gives managers the flexibility to rotate individuals in and out of marketing activities according to their 'real' paying client work. It also allows you to see how much time the business spends on sales and marketing, and therefore allows you to plan more effectively what your sales and marketing investment needs to be.

Recovery unpacked

Once you've established the principle above, per cent recovery is easy. It's simply this:

Of the available billable hours, what percentage was billed to clients (at the correct rate)?

If yours is the kind of service business that invoices its clients based on timesheets, this percentage should be hovering around 100 per cent. If it's lower, then you are over-servicing your clients compared to what they are paying – this is usually down to either mis-estimation, inefficient project management or slow delivery; each can be addressed through training. If it's higher, you are under-servicing them and, while it means more short-term profit, eventually the affected clients will catch on. Both require management intervention to correct the error.

	Available billable hours	2,721	100%
Utilisation	Hours of billable time used	2,420	89%
Recovery	Of which, hours actually billed	2,000	83%
Efficiency = U x R			**74%**

Putting them together: UxR

If on the other hand your clients pay fixed fees (either for services or for products), then this measurement gives you indications that you need to change things. This might involve improving estimating; it might also require speeding up production, adjusting quality or simplifying the product, lowering staff costs, reducing costs of sale, increasing prices and so on.

Putting them together

Each month UxR is reported, so the team can see if the company's management and billing processes are in sync. If utilisation is 100 per cent and recovery 100 per cent, then efficiency (UxR) is 100 per cent. This is the goal state.

If utilisation is 80 per cent and recovery 70 per cent, efficiency is just 56 per cent – clearly very far from ideal. The compounding of the two numbers forces problems into the sunlight. If there is a significant error in a given month, then the numbers can be unpacked and root causes identified and if necessary fixed. If there is a persistent error then the team can assign someone to come up with a robust solution, which may involve more radical changes than just tactical training.

At the beginning of this section I noted the strong connection between this formula and the staff costs-to-gross profit ratio. The two have a direct relationship: if utilisation is low, there is a direct effect on the desired 55 per cent – in fact, a lower utilisation means a higher staff cost and therefore higher ratio. A lower recovery means a lower gross profit and therefore a higher ratio. As a reminder, a higher-than-55 per cent ratio indicates staff are being under-worked, and a lower-than-55 per cent ratio indicates staff are overworked (more utilised hours than normally available in a standard day).

In effect, the staff/GP ratio is a super-KPI. However, until you have utilisation and recovery both nailed down, it would be unwise to abandon reporting it in the 2Y3X Roadmap session, as it provides such a useful management tool. As with many of the other measures, UxR is a wonderful indicator, as you get better, of the steady progress you and your team are making.

In practice this is quite a complex task to undertake, and it will take time to get right. This is usually either because the team neglects to tell colleagues exactly what is required, or because leadership sets a bad example by not doing timesheets. So you will need to do your timesheets too. Sorry.

Task

Month 1 – Research

- Determine what timesheets are being done currently and by whom, using what system.
- Select a time-tracking system.
- For each job role define hours available to be utilised on billable work.
- Work out how to reconcile billing to hours worked.

Month 2 – Prototype

- Communicate rationale and roll out timesheets to all staff.
- Reconcile actual customer billing with hours worked.
- Review utilisation hours for each role and refine available hours based on observations.

Month 3 – Implement

- Establish reporting at department level as well as for the GLT.
- Assign responsibility for internal education of managers to improve efficiency.
- Ensure data is included in product development and pricing reviews.

- Assign responsibility for overall company-wide improvement and management – this might be to a resource manager, head of customer service, head of production, or head of operations.

KEY TAKEAWAYS

- Planning ahead, facilitated by the Roadmap format, will save you a world of surprise and pain. This applies to cash collection methods as much as it does to forecasting when you will need to move premises.
- The two most overlooked KPIs are:
  - Staff cost-to-gross profit ratio, which for most service businesses should be around 55 per cent
  - Efficiency, which is the product of utilisation (how much of your staff's available time is spent on work paid for by the customer) and recovery (how much of the utilised time is actually paid for by the customer). Timesheets give you the data you need for this; blended rates make the data too poor to be really useful.
- Report your KPIs every month to the GLT. The team will learn the ins and outs of accounting and have the opportunity to interrogate and understand the data to improve decision-making.

7

Processes

Establishing continuity

In order to set all these new good disciplines in train, and so you don't have to keep doing them over, you will need to create a series of new processes. These will underpin how you now do things in your company. These processes will define the resources required so the GLT is not the bottleneck. There will be new manuals for how you interview, assess progress, approach sales, measure efficiency, even maintain profits. As you grow, the way you implement, document and most importantly keep alive these processes will define how quickly and surely you can scale.

The quarterly tasks in the People, Customers, Sales and Marketing, and Corporate and Finance segments can be defined, and often easily delivered by the GLT – in practice most of them will require new processes that will be continued by people outside this team. The

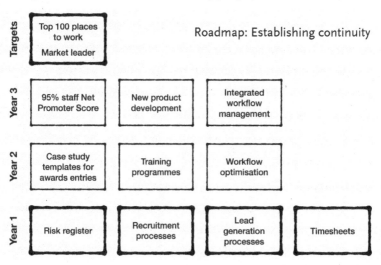

Roadmap: Establishing continuity

Targets	Top 100 places to work Market leader			
Year 3	95% staff Net Promoter Score	New product development	Integrated workflow management	
Year 2	Case study templates for awards entries	Training programmes	Workflow optimisation	
Year 1	Risk register	Recruitment processes	Lead generation processes	Timesheets

processes themselves will still have to be initiated by your GLT, so they can subsequently be delegated to the most appropriate departments for continuing use.

For example, the three-part formula, *utilisation* x *recovery* = *efficiency*, requires accurate information to be gathered. Without data on who worked for how long on which project, product or service, you cannot gauge utilisation. Without accurate billing information you can't gauge recovery. Timesheets are therefore going to be a necessity. A project to implement timesheets may therefore become an early quarterly task, as UxR cannot be done without it. This task will fall under the Processes heading in the Strategy Map.

A weighted pipeline also requires some processes to be implemented: measuring current leads/sales-qualified leads/pitches/quotes/decisions awaited, then accurately weighting them (with a secondary process of evaluation for continuous improvement) and reporting them.

Other new processes include those around HR: hiring pipeline, interviewing and reference checking, onboarding, scorecards, continuous development etc; customer satisfaction surveys; employee engagement, etc. While these will be uncovered within the strategic work in the 2Y3X Roadmap, the processes that support the new policies will need to be designed separately, and should be listed in this section. You will find that some juggling is required once you start populating the Process segment with tasks, as the catch-all 'Hiring strategy' in the People segment may include several processes for this segment, including 'Implement a recruitment CRM' and 'Set up a monthly designers-who-code coffee morning'.

Where a new process is designed and implemented, someone outside the growth lab team should then be made responsible for rolling it out – training, monitoring, improving and reporting on it. This person will usually be the head of the department concerned (e.g. head of sales, HR director, head of IT), who will then own the process as the company expands. This is a direct example of the scaffolding-for-future-growth nature of the 2Y3X Roadmap work.

More than any other area, the Processes segment requires good design. Why? The processes you design and implement here are not discretionary, and once implemented are not easy to improve or replace. Each process will be 'the way we do things around here' for a number of years to come. As such, while it may look like simplicity itself to implement a given Process task, in reality the Research phase becomes critical, and the Prototype phase should really test the mettle of the process being created. Don't be afraid of extending the delivery of a Process task over more than a single quarter. These are the ones you need to get right.

I will address just one Process task in detail here, the risk register, because unless you address it you may find yourself unexpectedly going out of business because you missed something dumb.

Risk register

A risk register is an often overlooked but incredibly useful tool. In essence it's a prophylactic against small things that could have big, potentially disastrous, consequences. One of my companies once won a contract from one of the country's biggest and most famous retailers. They presented their contract and without question (well, after we'd checked their supplier payment terms) we signed it. What a coup! Only later, on compiling our first ever risk register, did we discover we were already in breach of contract. We'd signed up to maintaining £1 million of professional indemnity insurance. When we checked we actually had a tenth of that.

Later in my career we had to consider major external threats to our business: terrorism which could shut down transport in our home city, London; the spectre of epidemic that could keep staff at home. These things are possible threats to our business. We wanted to at least have considered them.

When there's the danger of something going wrong, your ability to assess the degree of possible damage comes down to whether you've got any information about it. In fact, there is a spectrum at play. At one end is uncertainty, where you're not sure what the danger is and you don't know what the consequences might be. In essence, a total lack of data. At the other end is risk. Risk is where you know what the danger is and you have some data to indicate what the consequences will be, and some data on how to prevent or mitigate the problem. Ideally you want to be at the risk end of the spectrum – because you can manage risk – and not at the uncertainty end of the spectrum, because you have no idea what to do about the unknown unknowns.

Outside work I used to fly gliders – 15-metre-wingspan aircraft without engines. It's a beautiful sport, and I used to love spending my summer weekends soaring above the glorious English countryside, occasionally landing in some field far from home. The aim was always to fly back to my home airfield in the Cotswolds. This sport – graceful, serene, exhilarating – is largely a volunteer sport. Instructors give their time to club members, and the airfield is operated and managed by members who aren't flying. Few are pros. An airfield is a busy, bustling place, with gliders being launched by winch or towed behind a powered plane, gliders coming in to land (more or less accurately near the launch point), tow vehicles manoeuvring, signal lights and signal calls ... think *Top Gun*'s aircraft carrier flight deck, only near-silent and set in the English countryside.

On an airfield there are risks. Most of the risks involve risk of death. In our bucolic gliding world we need to avoid this at all costs, of course. But because of the volunteer nature of the sport, it's impossible to expect that everyone on the airfield knows what to do in an emergency. So we have a series of simple, well-illustrated manuals. They cover things like how operate the tow trucks, or replace frayed winch cables. But most importantly they give simple lists of what to do in emergencies. A single sheet covering every eventuality: if it happens there's a process for it. Nobody has to think; you just follow the directions.

This prepared crib sheet is incredibly well thought through. At Aston Down airfield, if there is any kind of medical emergency (from winch operator injury to a bad landing), one of the items on the laminated list of what to do instructs all the airfield gates to be opened so emergency vehicles won't be impeded no matter which direction they come from. Would you have thought about that? I worked on that airfield every summer weekend for several years. It wouldn't have occurred to me until the sirens were audible.

This kind of thinking stems from knowing that things can and sometimes do go wrong. It asks: 'If it does happen, what needs to be done?' It takes away the requirement for clear thinking in a crisis. Nobody has to remember all of the things; it's written down.

Creating a risk register for your company compels this pre-thinking. It forces you to address everything, big to small, from losing 40 per cent of your business overnight because of a screw-up to losing the one person who knows how to operate your credit control system or your safe.

The risk register isn't always about such existential threats. It should cover as much as possible that could affect the people in the business or the business itself. And while few if any of the threats may ever come through, it provides a huge degree of comfort, and ultimately safety, to know that in a crisis there is already a plan of action.

On the following page is a list of risk register topics compiled for a company I chaired a few years ago. I am indebted to one of my trusted colleagues, Julie Fawcett, who has worked with me as a super-smart consulting finance director across several businesses. Julie's eagle eye has uncovered too many risks to count, and her diligence in helping people prepare for the worst has saved much stress and probably a company or two. Set an exercise for the task's owner to decide what to do about them.

- Are there any suppliers you are reliant on? Do you have contracts? With service levels? Penalties if breached?
- Borders and immigration rule changes: impact on hiring staff?
- Cash flow: contingency plans if big clients don't pay on time.
- Change of government.
- Client contract breaches: if at present there is no central log of client contracts, it is impossible to know if you are in breach.
- Client contracts – or lack of – means if there is a dispute it will be harder to resolve.
- Client goes bust.
- Client satisfaction: could result in the loss of a client or loss of potential client due to word of mouth.
- Competitors stealing market share.
- Compliance: Legal/regulatory awareness/understanding/ changes; ignorance is not a defence.
- Contingency access to bank accounts.
- Currency movements.
- Data protection registration.
- Fraud: at present X has sole control over payments, and cybercrime is increasing.
- GDPR: proof of protection must be verified.
- Health and safety policy/compliance (first aid, fire officer, electrical certification, etc.)
- Incident that causes disruption to systems, facilities, staff, such as a fire, cyber-attack, terrorist event.
- Lack of staff: what if they leave, are sick?
- Lack of travel insurance for staff.
- Loss of biggest client.
- Loss of knowledge when staff leave.
- Loss of personnel, especially CEO: who would make all the decisions (operational and legal).

- Morale: high staff turnover, difficulty hiring.
- PAYE (pay-as-you-earn) tax audit.
- Signing of unfavourable client contracts.
- Staff/freelancers/clients/suppliers taking your intellectual property (IP) and using it without your approval, or giving it to competitors.
- Unlicensed software.
- Employment law: are our employment contracts legally binding?

There are of course many other things that could and possibly should go on this list, and some of them will be peculiar to your location, industry or company. The top five threats might warrant inclusion in your company's SWOT as well.

As a quarterly task the risk register is not particularly exciting for some people, and yet I've never had a group where a volunteer for this hasn't been quick to put their hand up. The research phase is quite simple, and starts with the above list. I would suggest the person who takes this on asks a variety of roles in the company for their list of possible risks: nobody knows all of them, and someone in IT or manufacturing or personnel will come up with things that wouldn't occur to you in a month of Sundays.

Once you have compiled a good list, you should rate each risk for impact, time to address, cost to address and urgency. Anything that could threaten your company's existence should obviously go to the top of the list. Once you have a prioritised list you can assign the task of addressing each risk into the company.

The risk register should become a living document, regularly updated and added to each time a mistake happens or anyone has a new contribution to make to it. It should probably be reviewed at least once a quarter by someone responsible, like the COO or FD.

Task
Month 1 – Research

- Gather existing internal lists of contingency plans.
- Research risk registers for your industry.
- Figure out a rating system for your risks. Red/amber/green is good as a prioritiser; it should take into account the likelihood of a given risk versus its impact on the business to indicate the urgency of addressing it. See the urgency-versus-importance table at the end of the section on the SWOT. You may also want to cross-reference the SWOT itself with the risk register.

Month 2 – Prototype

- Draft list.
- Draft red/amber/green calculator and highlight most urgent actions.
- Identify who will take responsibility for this going forwards.

Month 3 – Implement

- Complete list and assign actions to address the greatest risks to individual staff and set deadlines for completion.
- Hand over ownership and responsibility for the risk register to the relevant senior member of staff.

KEY TAKEAWAYS

- Most Roadmap tasks will result in new or revised processes. These must become the way you do things in your company from now on. You will need to design processes in such a way that they can be rolled out by people in your wider business, then kept alive and to the required standards for your next stage of growth.
- The risk register is a critical element of your preparedness for future emergencies. This will cover everything from what to do in a pandemic to what happens if the Internet goes down, fuel prices go up, you make a supply mistake, or you have to expand in a hurry. Get your risk register in shape sooner rather than later.

8

Bringing It Together

Full Strategy Map

Here is a reminder of what the Strategy Map looks like when fully fleshed-out.

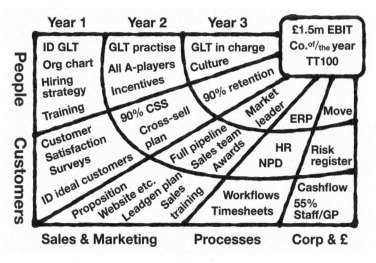

Full Strategy Map

Obviously your own will be substantially different from this in many areas, especially in its targets, Sales and Marketing and the later stage of the Customer segment. Most companies I've worked with share many of the People, Process and Corporate tasks.

Once completed, the GLT will debate the order and priority of each task indicated for Year 1, noting interdependencies and any priorities imposed by the company's SWOT. The tasks will then be mapped in the 2Y3X Roadmap itself.

Full Roadmap

Q1	Q2
Hiring strategy	Job scorecards
Proposition	Website, materials
Timesheets	ID low-profit vs ideal clients
Cust. satisfaction survey	Account Manager training
Low-profit clients up or out	Staff engagement survey
Lead generation activity	Sales training
55% Staff Costs to GP ratio	Staff training programme
Right people on the bus	ID workflows to optimise
Q3	**Q4**

Full Roadmap

Once the 2Y3X Roadmap has been compiled from the Strategy Map, the GLT will decide who will take responsibility for delivering each task in Q1. While it might be tempting to allocate tasks for the whole year, in reality some tasks will change and may be recalibrated to span two or more quarters. At the same time, it can be a great learning experience for individual team members to take on tasks outside their current comfort zone, and in fact, eventually all tasks will be brand new to the team.

Q1

Hiring strategy	Peter
Proposition	Kelly
Timesheets	Samira
Cust. satisfaction survey	Joe
Low-profit clients up or out	
Lead generation activity	
55% Staff Costs to GP ratio	
Right people on the bus	

Q2

Job scorecards
Website, materials
ID low-profit vs ideal clients
Account Manager training
Staff engagement survey
Sales training
Staff training programme
ID workflows to optimise

Q3

Q4

Full Roadmap with Q1 tasks assigned

Once a task has been allocated, the group must take care to clearly define what is expected at each of the Research, Prototype and Implement phases of each specific task. As each task is defined, make detailed notes of the expectations, and as good delegation practice make sure the task's owner repeats back to the group what they have heard and what they will be delivering.

Meeting rhythms

As a leader I was always a bit unpredictable, which made it hard for people who didn't know me to have faith I could deliver. It wasn't a great management style. I really didn't understand for the longest time that people yearn for predictability and not the excitement of the unknown! I never really established a regular schedule, and it frustrated many of the supremely talented people in my team. My mentor Charles Llewellyn finally introduced the idea of meeting rhythms as the reliable beating heart of a business, fifteen years after I'd started my first. Very swiftly indeed these were delegated to the management team and, lo and behold, the company immediately benefitted from the predictable (but for me unforeseen) calm.

Meeting rhythms ground people, providing stability. They manage expectations and allow people to defer issues until an appropriate time without guilt or stress. A simple, well-structured schedule means that issues can be addressed in time to head off bigger problems. If someone is off sick, you'll know at the beginning of the day, not when they don't show up to your critical customer meeting. If a project needs more resource, then knowing it a month before delivery or a week before the next stage is defined means customer expectations can be managed or more staff brought in to speed things up.

If, like the Strategy Map, we start at the biggest picture and work backwards, then a simple meeting rhythm might look like this:

- Three-year strategy review and forward planning. Annual. Two days.
- 2Y3X Roadmap review and forward planning. Quarterly. One day.
- 2Y3X Roadmap progress update. Monthly. One day (including training).
- Growth lab check-in. Weekly. One hour.
- Department-level updates. Daily. Twenty minutes.

This meeting rhythm, like the Strategy Map itself, is fractal. You can use this for all sorts of big picture-to-little picture management structures, project progression, personal development plans and so on. My advice is to not over-complicate things, but also to create predictability within your company: no-one likes surprises, and everyone wants to know where they stand. Having a predictable, normal meeting cadence gives reassurance.

Because the 2Y3X Roadmap has several tasks on the go at any given time, and many of these require collaboration between GLT members as well as different departments, part of the weekly growth lab check-in should be devoted to making sure teammates participate fully in decision-making and opinion-gathering. While the monthly Roadmap days are for deeper shared progress updates and facilitated decision-making, the weekly catch-ups will ideally deal with all operational aspects of tasks. As a consequence, GLT members should be able to come to the monthly meeting fully prepared with agreed directions and conclusions and well-prepared next steps.

Agenda for the Roadmap day

Here is the agenda for the 2Y3X Roadmap session. It doesn't really change from month to month other than for the quarterly reviews. In practice we usually start the day with an hour for the owners, discussing any strategic non-Roadmap issues like M&A, personnel, unexpected opportunities or threats, before we convene the 2Y3X Roadmap meeting. Afterwards we will generally run a training workshop and individual coaching or mentoring sessions if time permits, but the rump of the day looks like this:

- Good news update
- Financials
- Key performance indicators
- Roadmap item-by-item review
- Deeper dive into one or more items
- Review of quarter's progress
- *End of every quarter: review of quarter's tasks and ongoing task implementation; preview next quarter, define task parameters and monthly milestones; review total progress to date*
- AOB (any other business arising from the session)
- Training

Having set aside time before the 2Y3X Roadmap session for a quick catch-up with the owners on strategic or board-level issues, this leaves around three hours for the 2Y3X Roadmap session itself, an hour or two for additional training, and an hour for mentoring of the owners or members of the GLT. That's a very intense day!

Let's explore each key agenda item.

Good news update

Opening board and roadmap progress meetings with good news is a good idea for several reasons:

- It allows a team of people, who may rarely get together, to update each other on small, large or personal triumphs so the whole team can acknowledge and celebrate those involved.
- It starts the session on a positive note, with the team feeling a sense of joint progress and positive collaboration.
- It shares information within the team that may not have made it across the business – in other words, a small triumph at department level which may have got lost in the larger news that circulates naturally.
- As an external advisor and chair, I get to hear the company's good news from the people involved, rather than just the headlines in the press or in the management accounts.

I like seeing the people I work with take pride in their achievements, big and small. And I love the shared reconnecting over good news, in a room that is just about to get down to the nitty-gritty of reporting the good and bad of finances, KPIs and roadmap tasks. A positive start sets the tone for the rest of the session, girds against any negatives or gnarly issues coming up, and makes everyone happy.

I think that's important. Board meetings (and I often work with companies that combine the board and Roadmap meetings) usually start with disposing of the previous month's minutes. Kicking off before that with good news enforces the notion that these meetings are about how to succeed, not just how to report the past.

Financials

I believe in transparency. Your senior team knows when things are going well, and they know when things aren't going so well. But they may not actually understand how a P&L works. I've come across so many employees who genuinely believe profit to be 'what lines the owner's pockets'. So I am a firm believer in educating people, sharing the pains and the joys, and having a plan for each eventuality.

It all comes back to inclusion: it's difficult to build a team that owns the outcomes of activities if they don't understand what those outcomes mean for the business. It's easy to say more sales equals more success equals more growth, but much more difficult to see success and growth and profit and not assume that the profit goes straight into the owner's boat fund. This is an unfortunate and unintended consequence of the traditional P&L format – whatever is left over is the profit, and that's the owner's. And there is absolutely no incentive for employees, even (or especially) senior staff, if they think they're shovelling money at the founders.

This problem is traditionally met with the old carrot and stick: bonuses if they hit targets, headcount reductions if they don't. In my experience this is counterproductive, and makes the CEO's job one of trying to balance morale with growth. How many times have you changed the bonus structure? How many times have you reached into your own pocket to pay bonuses or even salaries when the company couldn't afford them, but employees expected them?

Far easier is transparency. The simple fact is that if you want to grow your company fast you will need to reinvest your profits. If you want a safety net to cope with the usual swings of business fortune, you will need to save some of the profits. If you want to take advantage of new opportunities, you will need cash from profits at hand. So if you have a plan for fast growth that requires profits to be reinvested or saved, then it is much easier to have your team build the plan around your ambitions. You must then keep them apprised of the financial details so they can calibrate additional tasks accordingly. In the monthly growth lab you are sharing information about the fortunes of the company with the people responsible for delivering the growth from now on.

The following approach to thinking about the P&L makes it much easier to communicate the needs of the business. GLT members will quickly see the effect they are having on the business's success as they take on Roadmap tasks and deliver more efficient systems and processes.

Profit & loss for the team

Here's a quick reminder of what a P&L looks like usually:

		Example	KPI
Sales or Turnover		200	
Less Cost of Sales	Less	(14)	
Gross Profit or Revenue	**Subtotal**	**186**	
Staff Costs	Less	102	**55%**
Overheads and Fixed Costs	Less	47	
Office costs			
Legal, accountancy, consultants			
Software, hardware, furniture etc.			
Net Profit or Operating Profit	**Remaining**	**37**	**20%**

Profit & Loss

Most people view this as being instructional, as in: take sales, less cost of sales, less staff, less overheads, and what you have left is profit.

This is how accountants tend to produce reports. Indeed, this is how you'll see reports in software or SaaS packages like the supremely usable Xero: it relegates profit to the end. As we discussed in the previous section, in order to deliver a decent balance in the bank that gives us a modicum of safety in the face of unforeseen fluctuations in sales, production or debt collection, we do need to be generating cash. Cash comes from profit. The formula shown above tells us that we need to make a certain amount of profit to put a sufficiently comfortable amount of cash in the bank. If we don't want to grow achingly slowly then we need to be generating 20 per cent profit from our activities for the safety net in the first year, and then investing what we can over and above maintaining a safety net of 3x monthly costs as our costs grow in line with revenue growth in accelerating growth through new initiatives.

In effect, 20 per cent is the minimum amount we need to do what we want to do. One way of protecting this profit is to put it at the top of the P&L table, rather than at the bottom:

		KPI	Example
Sales or Turnover			200
Less Cost of Sales	Less		(14)
Gross Profit or Revenue	**Subtotal**		**186**
Net Profit or Operating Profit	Less	**20%**	**37**
Remaining for Staff and Overheads	Subtotal		149
Staff Costs	Less	**55%**	102
Overheads and Fixed Costs	Remaining		47
Office costs			
Legal, accountancy, consultants			
Software, hardware, furniture etc.			

Profit & Loss for the team

This way the first thing you set aside is the profit. Once you've done that, set the staff cost so it sits at 55 per cent of gross profit. You have now used 75 per cent of your gross profit.

Whatever you have left is therefore available for overheads, or for additional profits that can be spent on strategic activities, including R&D, innovation, investment, expansion into new territories or acquisitions.

This approach forces you to think economically. It encourages finding lower-cost rather than flashier offices, immediate economies of scale if you acquire businesses and a focus on reducing unnecessary expenses. In fact, if you can reduce your overheads significantly, everything that is left over gets added to your available profits and can be spent on more rapid expansion.

I would teach all this to the growth lab team. If they are the superstars you think they are, and they're destined for great things like running their own companies one day, they'll have to learn it all sooner or later, and this way you will encourage business thinking early in their development.

Having the finance director in the room

Because of this, if your company has a finance director (even if that person only comes in a couple of days a month to review the work of the finance manager or bookkeeper) they should be in the Roadmap meeting. Why? Because a finance director will have the management accounts on hand ready for KPI reporting and can unpack and explain any numbers that are abnormal, confusing or which have practical implications.

While the Financial Director (FD) may not be strategic in their own role, part of their job is to provide decision-making support to the CEO when decisions need to be made. This may include finding funding to resource some new activity (i.e. training), reducing costs to meet reductions in sales due to a refinement in product offering, or planning a year ahead for an office move.

Rather than the CEO simply summarising team decisions and the FD delivering the necessary based on a summary brief, having them in the room means they can understand the context for decisions, have advance notice of decisions that may have consequences some months or years ahead, and so plan accordingly.

Having your FD in these meetings means actions that have financial implications can be discussed and often as a result agreed on the spot. It is invaluable having their specialist, practical perspective when it comes to the realistic planning of actions, many of which will require resourcing and financing.

Exposure to the FD means the growth lab team has an opportunity to learn how the financial mechanisms of your company work. Its members will at some point be managing the company; the earlier they learn the better.

And finally, the more familiar they become with the constraints and obsessions of the finance department, the less they will view them as the enemy who just gets in the way of investment. Building familiarity between the FD and the GLT will quickly oil the wheels of progress and change.

KPIs

Key performance indicators (KPIs) come in a number of flavours. You will probably have seen reports diving into huge detail on every aspect of production, throughput, sales ratios, cash flows, return on capital, gross margin percentage, etc. After I'd wrestled cash flow into shape in my early career I tried very hard to get my head around all this, but found it more of a distraction than anything else. In the early days all I really had to worry about was cash flow and sales; later the focus shifted to projecting sales and managing headcount to deliver the work. Profit was just what was (occasionally) left.

Once I'd had a few failures, and a few successes, I realised that while it is indeed critical that the managing director and finance staff had an iron grasp of the fine details, these KPIs weren't that useful to the broader management team, some of whom are neither financially literate nor interested. At the end of the day do you need the best creative in the world to be able to navigate a spreadsheet? Not so much.

After trying all sorts of reporting structures and frameworks, the conclusion my various teams came to was that a KPI should be a real and important indicator. If it indicates normalcy or tracks to what we have designed and expect, then great, no need to look further. However, if is off-track then we can dive in and unpack it at team level. It is an indicator that points to things we may need to understand. This is both positive and negative. If the KPI says you're doing better than expected, then it is worth unpacking it a little to see if there is an obvious explanation so we can try to repeat it. If worse, then understanding the cause is critical so it can be addressed and something be done about it.

This is similar to what happens in the financial reporting section of a board meeting. If profit is low, then we can assume costs or expenses are high compared to throughput and/or pricing is lower than required. The management accounts can be dug into and the problem area exposed, a solution discussed and actions agreed.

Performance indicators use data to highlight areas for attention. Key performance indicators are the highest-level numbers that tell the wider growth team whether there's something that needs to be addressed. They also help to tell each department in the company what is most important. The management truism is that what gets measured gets done.

Each of these KPIs should be familiar to you by now, so you will know how to derive the numbers, what sits beneath them, what actions might be implied, and how to deal with specific issues you are likely to encounter. In the meantime here is a quick summary of the KPI report:

Staff/GP ratio

- Target 55 per cent or equivalent.
- Anything below 55 per cent causes overwork and stress. If forecast, then you should plan something morale-boosting to

acknowledge and defuse it. Anything above 55 per cent indicates either overstaffing, bad resource allocation or wasted profit.

Utilisation x Recovery

• Target 100 per cent.

• The percentage of timesheet-allocated available billable hours (defined for each role) multiplied by the percentage of billable hours worked and billed to the customer gives your efficiency.

• If the figure is lower than 100 per cent, given a tolerance to be agreed by your team, then you can examine the underlying numbers and address the causes.

• The monthly report should be supported by the underlying statistics, so you can dive in if required by a worse-than-desirable headline number.

Client satisfaction score

• Target 90 per cent or higher average aggregate score.

• Headline number is average score aggregated across all possible responses.

• Supporting pages/slides showing each client's scorecard. This allows you to review any issues if necessary, or highlight specific growth or innovation opportunities.

Client satisfaction survey percentage of respondents

• Target 100 per cent.

• Exceptions to be highlighted.

Client satisfaction trends report

• 13-month line chart of headline score.

• 13-month line chart of aggregate score by client.

- 13-month bar chart of high-low score range by question. This will highlight any problem areas as well as eventually giving us a long view on whether there are predicated peaks and troughs during the year.

Weighted sales pipeline value

- Target £ to be established.
- Overall value of new business pipeline weighted using stage, likelihood, proximity to being closed; and 10 per cent, 50 per cent, 90 per cent splits.

Number of leads

- Target number to be established.
- If you have X leads as determined from past data, then you will generate the required number of Y meetings this month.

Number of prospect meetings

- Target number to be established.
- If you have this many meetings this month, you will have the required number of pitches (Z) this month.

Number of pitches

- Target number to be established.
- If you have this many pitches this month, you will have the required volume of sales (£) this month.

Conversion (or pitch-to-win) ratio

- For B2B pitches this should be target 50 per cent plus, but this will be determined by channel, sector and market norms. Regardless, set this high!
- Indicates whether sales training, product fit or pricing should be reviewed.

13-month rolling charts

I am an intensely visual person: if it can't be drawn in a pretty picture then it's rare that I will understand it first time round. That's one of the reasons I love the Strategy Map. And if you were to see me in my natural working environment of the boardroom, you wouldn't fail to notice the whiteboards, flip charts and stickies I insist on. In fact, if you were there, you'd be more than likely to see me drawing diagrams in fat blue marker, explaining some abstract idea in pictures. During the COVID-19 lockdown one of the first things I did for continuity was set up my iPad and Pencil as a virtual whiteboard for use in videoconference workshops!

I am also conscious that not everyone is like me, and that for other people different ways of taking in information – narrative, lists, numbers, practising or hearing – are way more effective. And of course, many people learn best by simply doing the thing they want to learn. In my case it takes several repetitions, which can be slightly boring if you have to wait for a new company to practise on each time. As such, one of the reasons we have a Q-Zero in the 2Y3X Roadmap process is to give people the chance to learn by doing.

However you prefer to take in information, one neglected aspect of information is that of comparison. We often look at a P&L and compare last month to the prior month, or to all of the months of the year up to the reporting date. What we seldom do is compare the latest report with the report from the same time in previous years. This would be useful – over time we would be able to see trends and fluctuations in various measures like revenue or profitability which may turn out to be a bit like standing waves, roughly consistent year in year out. If we could see this, we'd be able to plan for it next time – perhaps to head it off with intensified marketing activity, or fewer freelancers, or scaling spend on bonuses or training proportionally to expected income.

As a start, I would strongly recommend that when you present monthly reports to the team and elsewhere, you compare the current month to the same month from the previous year. The simplest way to do this is to use a thirteen-month rolling report format, so that if you are in October then last October is also in view. This applies as much to a P&L report as to client satisfaction scores, UxR, staff costs/GP, cash flow, sales pipeline and recruitment pipeline. (Your FD will probably point out that they do this for the balance sheet already.) It doesn't matter whether it's numbers in a table (P&L, etc.) or a line chart, though given that each member of your team will most easily take it in in different ways it would be sensible to present the information in a variety of formats. This should include having the person presenting the information reading it out and explaining it as they go . Not only does this give everyone an opportunity to ask questions, but it also encourages the presenter to really understand what they're sharing with their colleagues.

2Y3X Roadmap review

Each item in the 2Y3X Roadmap gets around fifteen minutes for the relevant item owner to report their progress. Good meeting practice dictates that any pre-reading has been circulated before the 2Y3X Roadmap day so that everyone is up to speed; any decisions required from the growth lab team have been sought in advance; and any research, prototyping or implementation has been done. In fact, as you'll have gathered from the notes on meeting rhythms, pretty much everyone should already be up to speed.

It should therefore be treated as a progress report, as opposed to a canvassing of opinions. The only exceptions are when a task needs to change from its original specification, either because the first month's research has shown that a different direction is required, or because the prototyping stage has brought to light something that will either curtail the project or extend it into an additional quarter (and therefore have an impact on other dependent tasks or resources).

In practice, every company and every individual growth lab

member will approach this differently. I've seen five beautifully presented decks in a row at one company, then the next day had five entirely different updates, ranging from a five-minute verbal update to a half-hour demonstration of a new KPI presentation tool. Over time the process will tighten, team members will become better presenters (especially if the chair builds in a mechanism for evaluating individual reports at the very end of the 2Y3X Roadmap session – 'Rachel's presentation today, was there anything she did brilliantly? Any tips on what might work even better?'), and the sessions will start to feel slicker. Bear in mind that if topical training is identified – e.g. presentation training – it can be added as an action either for the traditional management workflow or for HR to undertake.

You may decide before you start which Roadmap item would benefit from further discussion or some specific training. The advantage of having the session chaired by an experienced external advisor who has had their own companies is that inevitably they will be able to provide shortcuts to some of the tasks, and wisdom to know when to employ them. It is usually very useful to expand on one task. This will expose the task's ins and outs to the rest of the team, provoking questions and discussion, and may prompt new thinking around other tasks or in regard to post-delivery companywide roll out.

It is important that the 2Y3X Roadmap session delivers tasks required by the Strategy Map. There is a risk that we put a great deal of effort into delivering a well-executed task, put the resulting manual into a drawer, and never think of it again. Thought must be given to how, once an item has been delivered, it will then be implemented by the company as a whole and, more importantly, how it will become 'the way we now do things around here'. This should be considered all the way through the research and prototyping phases of the task, so that the task is delivered with implementation designed into it.

Where help is required to take a delivered task and build it into the company's processes and culture, this should be sought from relevant managers or talent outside the GLT. For this reason, among many others, it's important that the 2Y3X Roadmap process is not hidden from the rest of the company.

Concluding the meeting

The conclusion of the session should be free for anyone to raise anything important with the team. This often sees issues raised by a more junior member of the team wishing to air something at a forum where everyone – including the boss – is equal. Some of my favourite moments have been when a junior superstar has questioned the order of things and raised an issue about a topic usually dealt with from on high. In fact, the satisfaction a good leader gets from seeing their perceived authority questioned for valid reasons by someone who would otherwise never have the chance to do so is usually cause for celebration.

This part of the meeting can also be used to air controversial issues, where the presence of an experienced external guide will render a potentially loaded discussion pragmatic and practical.

I usually finish by congratulating the team on its progress and setting the reading list for the next quarter based on what's coming up.

KEY TAKEAWAYS

- Never miss a Roadmap meeting. You will need a weekly GLT check-in, monthly Roadmap day (preferably facilitated), quarterly review and planning day, and annual strategy review and Roadmap planning day.
    - The agenda for the monthly Roadmap day is:
    - Good news update
    - Financials
    - Key performance indicators
    - Roadmap item-by-item review
    - Deeper dive into one or more items
    - Review of the quarter's progress

9

Emergency Planning

What to do when the unexpected strikes

One of my first clients when I started my consulting career, following the sale of my last company, was a business in dire straits. There were a dozen staff when we started, and the company was losing £70,000 a month. They adopted the programme, and over two years we more than doubled their revenue and got them up to 17 per cent net profit. That experience had shown me that the programme would work for turnarounds. The COVID-19 crisis called for a return to that turnaround mindset.

When the new crisis happened, we realised very quickly that most business owners didn't have a clue what to do first, last or at all. As a result, we threw open the doors of our consulting firm and went pro bono. We had a roster of experienced consultants, all of whom had weathered previous crises, including the unexpected industry collapse following the bursting of the dot.com bubble, the crisis of confidence following 9/11, and the deep recession after the banking collapse of 2008. We had all previously encountered the unexpected, coped with it, and come out stronger (or at least with some perspective). We felt this experience would be valuable to those newer entrepreneurs who simply had no idea which way to turn. So we made our experience available free of charge.

In some ways this was an extreme pivot: we turned on a dime and changed what we were doing literally over the course of a weekend. We made the decision without a plan, if I am completely honest; it just seemed like the correct thing to do. And, what else could we do? We certainly weren't going to be beefing up our marketing and trying to win new clients.

The effects were almost instantaneous, and entirely unpredicted. We found ourselves fielding approaches from industry heavyweights from all over the world, offering their services voluntarily to the business owners who came to us for help. These new relationships gave us an international pool of extraordinary talent, which we could train in the art of 2Y3X, scaling at speed. As part of this need to help the helpers, and in part thanks to their own experiences, we realised that this programme actually lends itself extremely well to an emergency. So with the expanding team's help we adapted it.

We developed a version of the 2Y3X Strategy Map framework that could be used for companies who, under the circumstances, couldn't plan long-term, but had to confront the situation at hand. During this extraordinary time, with the economy switched off for months (at the beginning we didn't know if it might be a few weeks or a year), owners needed direction. Some of course found themselves unable to do anything at all: balance sheet poverty or the imperative to furlough or lay off all staff meant a straightforward hiatus. But for others, this was a time to roll up their sleeves and address the new reality head on. The roadmap tool we developed, called the QuickMap®, was a simple response to this need.

The QuickMap

This new QuickMap is a smaller version of the Strategy Map. QuickMap works on the basis that we do a day's planning to start off with, again with the superstars of the business, and instead of addressing three years we develop a three-month plan.

We start at the end, and work backwards to fill in the gaps.

During the COVID-19 crisis we figured that the world would be starting to spin back up no sooner than three months hence. This was a pragmatic view: if it rebooted sooner then most businesses would survive and the new world would not be too unlike the way it had been before. More than three months would probably be damaging, and potentially transformative. And businesses would be likely to need a new plan of action so they could be ready once doors did start opening again. Even if the crisis were to last nine months, the business would be prepared for the rebound (even if the rebound were just a dead cat bounce).[14]

Having been there before, all of us at our firm were also aware that the other side of COVID was lurking a new and potentially brutal recession.

Working with our pro bono clients and our volunteer consultants we devised a simple set of goals for the end of the QuickMap period:

1. Incoming customers buying products or services that would be more or less recession-proof
2. A workforce prepared and ready for action

The QuickMap format is broken down into three months. The same focus areas remain: people, customers, sales and marketing, processes, corporate and financial. Each member of the GLT (newly assembled in many cases) has just one month to deliver each task, rather than three, and as a consequence the rigour of research, prototype and implement isn't available in the same way.

However, on the basis that this is an emergency turnaround plan rather than a medium-term strategic transformation, it doesn't matter. The tasks and actions need to be delivered fast. By necessity some of the work won't stand the test of time, but it's not there for that – it's there simply to effect preparedness for the immediate future. Once your firm is back to business as usual you can either revert to the original Strategy Map, revisit it and reconstruct it based on the new reality, or, if you haven't done one before, start from scratch, taking into account the new business baseline.

[14] https://en.wikipedia.org/wiki/Dead_cat_bounce

Here it's worth noting that, in my experience, recession is an extraordinarily rich time for new businesses. Almost all of my own startups were born when there had been a sweeping clear-out of inflexible businesses or industries. When you are facing a few years of hard recession, and what used to work no longer does, you have no choice but to look at what opportunities there might be through entirely fresh eyes. The only businesses that will work will be those that fit with the landscape before you. Recessions therefore require adaptability, and adaptability requires the ability and willingness to abandon the old plan if necessary and begin a new one. In the context of developing the normal three-year Strategy Map you will recall that getting the product/market fit right, getting the proposition right, understanding and mapping risks and building in resilience in case of crisis, constant checking in with customers about their needs, and so on, are all component parts of a well-constructed plan.

Back to the QuickMap. While the matter at hand is survival and a quick pivot to a new situation, you should make sure that whatever you are planning to be at the end of the next three months will fit the future role of the business. You must still think about what you will want to do once you have made it through the immediate crisis.

The highest priority is of course to sort out cash and profitability – the first by calling clients fast and ensuring credit control is well in hand, and the second by addressing number of staff and cost of overheads versus level of income. Having had to sell a company once under duress purely because we had failed to downsize fast enough in response to losing two major customers, I know not only how painful this can be, but also how dangerous inaction is. Of course, this forces your hand if you have not already addressed who you should and should not have on your team.

What else came up time and again during the creation of these QuickMaps during the crisis? Here is an example:

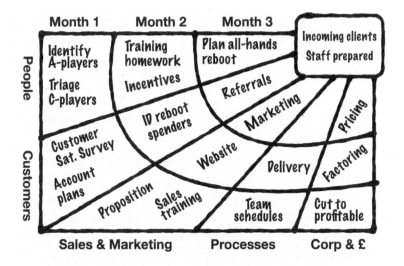

The QuickMap

As you can see, it is very similar to the Strategy Map, but with actions that can be executed fast and without a huge amount of new process. Again, core tasks include understanding customer needs, redefining proposition (especially in light of the situation likely to be in place *after* the three months is up), and marketing.

In addition, there's an imperative to get your staff lined up and ready for action. This may involve rapid training in new delivery workflows, or in new products more suited to the future than those that have fallen by the wayside. Important too is the need for management to shift staff roles and responsibilities perhaps temporarily in order to effect changes speedily.

Making it happen

In turning this plan of action into results, it is not good enough to just have a monthly Roadmap review day as with the two-year programme. Because this is a short-term emergency planning tool suitable for a radical or unforeseen pivot (or turnaround), it will necessarily require short interventions implemented fast. The usual month to dedicate to each stage – research, prototype and implement – is not available. You will therefore need to have much more frequent check-ins with your team. This schedule, or meeting rhythm, will be at pace:

1. Daily stand-up for the whole GLT (during COVID this was done via videoconference).

2. Weekly GLT review of each task, taking up to two hours once a week.

3. Task progress meeting every two weeks, with the first being a call to action in case additional help or resource is required and the second, part of the monthly day, being the completion report with next steps.

4. Monthly day reviewing the completed tasks, recalibrating the next set of tasks based on updated circumstances as necessary, describing resource needs for the coming month, and setting clear deliverables.

I would strongly recommend that you have an external consultant with experience of crisis management or fast turnaround action planning to hold you to account during this period, at least for each monthly review day. In between, you will need strong leadership to hold the team's feet to the flames and ensure each daily and weekly meeting is run without fail. This is a critical time, and consistent rhythm and rapid progress are crucial if you are going to be successful.

As such, you should remember that if any team member is unavailable for any meeting their report should be delivered by a proxy, who also takes responsibility for feeding back the group's comments to the task owner. In the daily stand-ups it may only take a couple of minutes for each member to check in; in the weekly meetings ten minutes each should suffice (on the understanding that one or more tasks may well require a bit more time).

At the end of the third month, a new session will be required to plan what comes next – either a new three-month sprint with a new QuickMap, or a day reviewing, updating or re-planning the overall Strategy Map. In fact, the QuickMap is great training for the 2Y3X programme itself.

What it means to lead in a crisis

This kind of emergency planning serves several purposes.

The first is to provide direction for leadership and the GLT, so that everyone can focus on a single-minded purpose even while chaos and uncertainty abounds. A floundering leader and strategic team will fail, almost certainly taking all hands with them.

The second is to give confidence to staff, to galvanise them into action, and reduce the risk of panic or, possibly worse, despondency. Good morale is terribly important, especially during uncertain times. Staff are likely to be worried about their job security, personal finances and what they tell their families. One of the things that became clear during the crisis we all went through was that neglecting people's sense of worth and security appreciably affected their continuing feeling of community. You are responsible, after all, for a company of people. All the camaraderie and water-cooler conversations, shared lunchtimes, gossip and congratulations or commiserations that happen by osmosis in an office environment are the essential (and invisible) medium for your company's culture. Good leadership means addressing this, through setting tasks that provide effective substitutes, while demonstrating a clear purpose and plan of action. This proactivity will help keep your people reassured, busy and forward-looking.

The third is to ensure the company's survival. The GLT needs to be decisive and work together as a team. It has to both deal with the immediate threats (cash, morale, customer retention, profitability), and make ready for the other end of the crisis. And having come up with a strategy and identified the tasks required to deliver it, the team has to pull together to make sure it's done. Once again, while any plan is better than no plan, any plan that is actioned is infinitely better than a plan left undone.

KEY TAKEAWAYS

- Use the ninety-day QuickMap format in an emergency to focus the team's minds on business-critical tasks. The emphasis should be on quick, practical actions – rolling your sleeves up – rather than nice-to-haves.
- It is usually best to have experienced external advisors to help you get through a crisis. They will provide perspective, wisdom and reassurance that you can and will survive.
- Provide leadership through decisive action: take charge but distribute responsibility; use the framework to provide context and stability.

10

Finally, How to Begin

Overcoming procrastination

Getting things done, whether during a crisis or once you have committed to a course of action, is the essence of leadership. You are the boss partly because you have proven yourself good at getting others to believe in your vision. Sometimes it's also because you are good at making decisions.

Some decisions are, of course, difficult. In the hierarchy of things to decide on, yours have the potential to break the company. Great decision-making isn't about always being right: it is about being prepared to *make* a decision even if it is wrong, having prepared to make a correction if necessary.

Procrastination happens when you know you have to make a decision but are not prepared to reverse it if you are wrong. Embarking on a programme like 2Y3X and implementing everything you have been reading about is a big deal. It is going to change the way you do things. It may even change the way you are as a leader. It will certainly change how your team works, and it will take your company to a different level altogether.

It is completely understandable to defer the decision to just get on with it to another day. There are, after all, an infinite number of readily available excuses: I'm not ready, the team is not ready, we don't have the money yet so let's just wait for the next big invoice to be paid, I can do it myself, the team can do it, there will be another one along in a minute...

We work with leaders of exceptional companies all the time. Most are really good at decision-making. All have their lapses into procrastination. So here are the five questions you need to ask yourself if you find yourself deferring the decision to start building your Strategy Map:

1. Do I know what we need to do?

This one is easy. Do your research into which system or programme you want to use, line up your best options and get your team to help you decide.

2. Will we really do it on our own?

If you believe this is the sort of thing that requires outside help to make it happen, get you going in the right direction or hold your feet to the flames, then this is the acid test. If you haven't done it already you probably need outside help. I would suggest 2Y3X, but then I'm biased.

3. Can we get someone in to do it?

If so, who's the best in the business, has the best references, has done it before, can nail it for you?

4. What is the price of getting it done?

In the grand scheme of things what is the value you'll get and what is the cost to get it, and what's the ratio in the short term and in the long term? If the project fee looks high but the value delivered is huge, think about it proportionately. Great companies charge by the value they deliver, not by the hour. (And incidentally, so should yours.)

5. What is the cost if we don't get it done?

Finally, what is the cost if you don't do it? Four more years? Two million less? Running aground on the next shallows? Never making your mark? Value has both positive and negative axes. Make sure you have enumerated both.

Ask yourself these five questions. Then stop procrastinating. Make the decision and let the next phase start now rather than waiting for it to happen in its own good time.

Getting help

Leadership can be a bit lonely.

Which is peculiar, since many leaders are extroverts, assertive ENTPs.[15] To their friends on Facebook they seem invulnerable, motivated, successful and popular. The famous loneliness at the top is not about the glory; it's about the responsibility. It's about the fact that ultimately the decisions have to rest on the shoulders of the leader, no-one else. It is you who has to hear the worst, to deal with the crises, to fire the popular laggard or patch up the client's ego. It's all on you.

The worst thing is, you can't share the stresses and strains. There is no-one you can offload to. Brett Fox wrote that the CEO's curse is that you can't tell your staff because it would freak them out; you can't tell your co-founders lest they think you weak; you can't tell your investors in case they lose faith; and you can't tell your spouse because they won't understand and you don't want to burden them. So you are stuck.

In the course of this book the idea of having some external reference point or advisor to hold you to account has come up several times. Having been a successful founder myself I do know how hard it is to stick to your own commitments – to the extent that sometimes you decide not to tell anyone about them, so you don't let yourself down in the eyes of those who look to you for an example. It makes life so much easier to have someone else to keep you on the straight and narrow. Your spouse can't do it (at least in this aspect of your life), and you are unlikely to want to hire someone that has more authority than you.

Thankfully you have options, though they can sometimes be confusing. How do you know whether you need a non-exec, a board advisor, chairperson, peer group or growth accelerator?

While I was still a co-founder and CEO, well before my career as a chairperson, I had spent fourteen years helping to pioneer digital comms, had done a couple of very high-profile corporate sales and, with

[15] See the somewhat controversial Myers Briggs Type Indicators (MBTI) at https://www.myersbriggs.org

the arrogance of relative youth and relative success, believed that I could do it all on my own. But as I've mentioned, bits kept falling off. I kept making mistakes – some catastrophic, some repeatedly. I didn't have anyone around me to do anything other than encourage me. And part of that was because I hid my inexperience and occasional ineptitude well.

After fifteen years as an entrepreneur I finally joined an organisation called Vistage, which operates in the UK and USA. Vistage runs peer groups of a dozen CEOs at a time, every member in a different industry, who meet once a month for soul-baring, note-comparing, solution-finding and, importantly, training. I discovered for the first time that I wasn't alone. And that every business has the same issues. I had honestly believed that digital was different, until a director of a global car manufacturer shared an issue they were experiencing that I, too – on a comparatively microscopic scale, of course – was finding troublesome. For me, spending a few thousand a year for professional development was unbelievably worthwhile. It gave me my education as a business manager, rather than just a sometimes-lucky entrepreneur.

This kind of peer-mentoring group can teach you how to do the job of running a business. I have taught on MBA courses at one of the world's best business schools and, believe me, such groups are better than any MBA for giving you practical, real-world exposure to the basics of general business management and leadership.

Confederations, institutes and industry bodies can also be useful. These are rarely as structured as Vistage or its equivalents. You won't do a regular day each month with the attendant personal coaching, but you can learn much about specific aspects of what it takes from your peers and competitors, and with teachers who understand the context of the business world.

When it comes to the loneliness and how to share the load with someone who both understands and can help, your options boil down to hiring a non-executive director, hiring a board consultant or consultancy, hiring a chairperson, or entering a programme. After I sold my last business I acted in all of these capacities and worked with dozens of companies that have been with others who do the same. In fact, most of the companies I work with now have had one or more of these before coming to my firm to capitalise on what they've learned along the way. More about that in a bit.

The non-exec is (usually) a respectable animal: sometimes long in the tooth, often grey-haired, semi-retired and motivated by a desire both to give back and to keep in touch. Proximity to entrepreneurs keeps the non-exec alive, because they too grew or helped grow a company and they know how stressful and exciting it is. It really is hard to leave the field. They know what it's like, often they have specific expertise relevant to a sector, and they can provide true wisdom and clarity of hindsight. This hindsight is invaluable. When you have an issue, they'll have seen it before and will know just what to do. Brilliant for response, usually very handy in a crisis. But, and it is a big but, they are tactical, not strategic. They can provide advice when you need it, if you ask for it, but you're still coming up with the strategy and the plan.

The chairperson is a slightly more proactive version of the non-exec. Becoming chair of the last company I sold was a great move for me, because I had a brilliant co-founder and an enormously experienced managing director running the business. As chair my role was industry-facing, building connections, working the corporate world so we were prepared for the strategic plays. It's a fun job. The chair holds the senior team to account. A really good chair will examine your strategy, test you on it, make sure you're prepared, and hold your feet to the flames. As HBR put it, 'The chair is responsible for and represents the board, while the CEO is responsible for, and is the public face of, the company.'

And they'll be your advocates within their own world. They'll represent you. For many of the firms I've chaired I've been a high-level go-between during M&A discussions, introducing the right lawyers, tax advisors and negotiators. They won't be your advisors so much as introducers and facilitators. Unlike the non-exec, however, the chair is rarely happy to take angst-ridden calls at 10 p.m. on a Wednesday evening because you've lost a key staff member. But without a chair, M&A becomes a debilitating distraction for the company's leaders.

And then there are the growth consultants. Not lead-generation 'specialists' (telemarketing agencies), but real, proper growth. These consultancies tend to have a finance-plus-marketing focus. Some also have a dedicated M&A function – and while they're often good, my own view is that when the time comes, M&A negotiations should be left in the hands of a firm that does nothing but that.

Typically they're run by people who have grown and sold a company or two themselves, and they are totally dedicated to showing you how to nail down your numbers and set some fundamental KPIs, and to helping you build a robust sales function. This two-pronged approach provides a significant platform for early- to-mid-stage growth. Simply by getting this stuff right will get you to a million or more in revenue on its own. It's basic, but utterly fundamental, and the consultancies know how best to get you there.

Finally, there's the structured programme. This is what I do now, working with companies with twenty-plus employees who want to create a structured, scalable business ready for major expansion. They have gone past the basics, usually have plateaued a little, already know the benefits of external advice, and are committed to more. Over the past few years almost all of them have doubled during the two-year 2Y3X Programme. Some have tripled in two years. Almost all those that didn't were acquired at a premium before they could complete the programme.

There are three reasons for all this success.

The first is that in order to know where you're going you need a guide who's been there themselves more than once, and knows the way clearly. They've seen the dots and can join them up. They can set appropriate intermediate goals and steer you around obstacles.

The second goes back to goal-setting theory, and the research which says that external feedback on each task is required to consistently achieve challenging goals. This applies no matter who you are in the growth lab team: future star or current CEO.

And the third is to do with commitment. All these companies have got to the point where the CEO's loneliness at the top and the utter and inescapable responsibility have worn a little thin. At the same time they've realised that they'll only enjoy serious success if their superstars are running the business alongside them, not just for them. The 2Y3X Programme is designed to build not just process but a genuinely great team, to distribute responsibility and distribute learning – to take the best of the great books you've read, to redistribute the load, and take the brakes off the people.

Because one of the biggest barriers to growth is the bandwidth at the top. The nature of concentrated responsibility and a command-and-control style means you can't afford to let six people do 20 per cent each in different directions, because you can't possibly maintain control. Your growth, no matter how good your marketing now is, is limited to you and by you.

I've been there and done it too.

The more committed companies go a slightly different way, and the end result is a well-designed workload spread among a coherent, cohesive and well-trained team of future superstars. Less stress and loneliness, greater shared responsibility. And, of course, massive growth.

KEY TAKEAWAY

- Now you've read the book you've got no excuse to procrastinate about what to do next.
- Get outside help. The perspectives and experience you will have on hand will mean sure-footed progress and scale at speed.
- Follow the 2Y3X methodology and your team will start sharing the load. Running your business will once again become a joy.
- All diagrams and illustrations in this book can be downloaded from https://scaleatspeed.com/illustrations/

Finally

The 2Y3X framework is incredibly tolerant of the experience or lack of it in the growth lab team. It works for six-person startups just as well as it does for hundred-person firms and groups of companies. It is also flexible in respect to the amount of time each task requires; in other words, you can take it as fast or as slowly as you wish.

In actual fact, by keeping the growth lab team to around six members, the pace of change in your company is likely to be entirely tolerable, especially if you have upgraded your people throughout your business. Yet you will be delivering the changes necessary for scaling your business: great people policies, customer focus, product improvement, sales capability, forecasting and financial strength. Over the course of the first two years you will have delivered perhaps thirty or forty strategically fundamental and lasting improvements. The scalability, even the immediate value, of your business will have skyrocketed.

The framework also builds incredible coherence, not only in terms of shared purpose and a guiding light throughout the company, but also within the growth lab itself. After a few months you will notice the team really does hold each member to account, actively expecting high standards on every task every month, while creating dialogue around difficult-to-define, -calibrate or -deliver task stages. This sharing of progress, of successes, of difficulties and solutions, creates an unbelievably tight team. When we lead clients through the managed programme (more on that at 2Y3X.com) this is one of the most satisfying aspects of the process.

And it yields what I believe is the greatest benefit: your freedom. You will have spread the load among a group of people who have become fanatical about the business. You will never again have to worry about being in the weeds. As the CEO of the world's leading luxury digital agency said to me:

> After nine months I suddenly realised I'd got my life back. It's all been on my shoulders since I started this company. It was always me working until midnight, me reaching into my pocket when we were short of cash to pay wages, my responsibility to carry the weight and the stress. That's all magically disappeared. I've got time for my girlfriend, my family, everyone around me is doing the right job and I'm happy for the first time in years.

This feeling seems to happen to everyone at around the nine-month mark, just when the team realises how much it has actually achieved together since they started the process. So perhaps you should give it a go. And right now might be the right time to take the first step.

Recommended Reading

Once upon a time I went on a speed-reading course: three days with an eccentric genius called Jan Cisek. During the course he showed us a variety of different techniques for consuming written material fast – really, really fast. We learned about (and practised) the I and T methods of scanning, using mind maps to make notes as we strip-mined perfectly well-written books, treating them like newspapers and so on.

I imagine Jan taught us so many different methods so that at least one or two would stick for each attendee. For me, scanning a book like a broadsheet works. So does the idea that every business book has around five core ideas in it, and if you open such a book and try and find those ideas in less than ten minutes, usually it's pretty easy. Why? Well, part of it is that most books are nicely laid out, with chapter headings and sections. And most publishers want more words than are strictly necessary to communicate the major points. A lot of business books are in fact mostly air.

You've just read 180 words that weren't strictly necessary, just as a preamble to me recommending a few gems that have shone out from the many, many books I've been able to get through as a result of Jan Cisek's great course. Here is my list of must-reads for anyone who really wants to build a brilliant company.

- *Good To Great* by Jim Collins
- *Scaling Up* by Verne Harnish
- *Who: The A Method for Hiring* by Geoff Smart & Randy Street
- *The Four Obsessions of the Exceptional Executive* by Patrick Lencione

- *Pitch Anything* by Oren Klaff
- *Never Split the Difference* by Chris Voss
- *Built to Sell* by John Warrilow
- *Scarcity: Why Having So Little Means So Much* by Eldar Shafir & Sendhil Mullainathan

This last one explains so much, and I found it a total revelation, despite it all being obvious common sense. Enjoy these books, buy lots of copies and keep them dotted around your company's offices for people to learn from.

Since the first edition of *Scale at Speed* was published, the 2Y3X programme has entered new markets in Europe, the Middle East, Africa and the US. As it should be, half the programme fee is dependent on at least doubling your revenue – although of course the principal aims of all of this are really about building a people-centred business.

Scaling requires transformative change as outlined in this book. The easiest way to effect change is to let the people most affected by it manage it. In fact, *Scale at Speed*'s approach can be most easily summarised as giving the task of designing the next version of your company to its future leaders, and helping them take it there.

This is the opposite of the old top-down, command-and-control method of management. The old way of running a business is no longer fit for purpose. With a clear view of what should replace it, my journey has continued and we now acquire companies and apply everything you've read here to create people-centred groups. We describe ourselves at AVA Acquisitions not as a holding company, but as a scaling company.

Our vision is: 'To empower rising talent to build the most inspiring agency network in the world.'

Our mission is even more practical: 'To give every agency team the tools to scale at speed.'

And that starts here, with this book, and with you.

I would strongly encourage you to look into the 2Y3X programme, which is in effect this book delivered for you. There are also Scale at Speed boardroom events and Scale at Speed mastermind groups that will help you implement everything you have read. Visit ScaleAtSpeed.com for information and to find out how to get in touch with your local group.

Finally, if you're curious about how your company compares to others on the same journey, there's a free self-assessment tool at ScaleAtSpeed.com/scorecard. This will tell you your score based on some of the metrics we use to evaluate companies for 2Y3X and as potential acquisitions for AVA, and it will help you identify what to prioritise as you plan your next steps.

Acknowledgements

I am supremely grateful to Kate Barker, my agent, who suggested I write this book in the first place and was endlessly patient as I did so. Kate came to me after hearing an interview by Lucy Mann on the SmallSparkTheory podcast.

Jim Sterne gave me an American perspective on my writing and provided encouragement and friendship from start to finish. Michael Nutley was incredibly generous with advice and editing, as was Celia Velarde – my mum, who gave me my appreciation for the written word – while my dad Giles taught me the power of the spoken. Tony Bond, Richard Kozma, Lincoln Exley and Tony Llewellyn lent their specialists' eyes; Tom Asker, my editor at Little, Brown, and Graham Coster gently illuminated the more complicated bits.

Over the years Jo Evans fed my love for negotiation and showed me the wonders of value pricing. Bryan Wilsher schooled me in finance. Jason Holland put up with my leadership mistakes for years and still inspires me.

Charles Llewellyn, Vistage chair and my first mentor, gave me the tools I lacked. He introduced me to many of the concepts and frameworks that led to my career as a specialist growth accelerator. Dag Andersson, Simon Birchenough, Rick Edmondson, Ali Karademir, Steve McNulty, Gareth Morris, Perween Warsi, Bill Williams, Gareth Warwick and others shared these early steps. Ali first introduced me to what evolved into the Strategy Map (and is now a member of our amazing team). Jim Alampi, creator of the 'Execution Maximizer', taught me the principles of his planning tools and was kind in his guidance when we discussed my evolving ideas a few years later.

Frank Kelcz and Mia McTigue-Rodriguez at our consulting firm 2Y3X (visit us at 2y3x.com) gave me space and support. Thanks too to Mo Lishomwa, Eva Appelbaum, Silvia Christmann, Owen Valentine Pringle, Georges Chakar, David Cushman, Jihad Al Houwayek, Sarah Vick, Polly Lygoe, Vonnie Alexander, Tim Deeson and Chris Averill; and to our amazing, brave, determined clients over the years for their faith in the process, and for the results.

Peter Lang, Tom Shipley, Jo Royce, Holly Flick and the incredibly talented team at AVA Acquisitions showed me what can be achieved just by empowering people to think bigger.

Behind the scenes Philippa Gebhardt, Axelle Fox, Sarah Vianney, Jim Credland, Helen Bowie and Katz Kiely kept me mostly sane, except when I was at Burning Man with Dan Lykken and our Sharkey's Bar & Lounge friends.

Finally, I am eternally grateful to Inna Bagoli Goncharenko, my lovely, amazing partner, who encouraged me and nourished me in every way, and then read and corrected the draft and still did it all again. Thank you.

Index